The 'Real' Spitfire Pilot

The 'Real' Spitfire Pilot

Flight Lieutenant D.M. Crook DFC's Original Unpublished Manuscript

Flight Lieutenant D.M. Crook DFC

Edited by Dilip Sarkar MBE

AIR WORLD

THE 'REAL' SPITFIRE PILOT
Flight Lieutenant D.M. Crook DFC's Original Unpublished Manuscript

This edition published in 2021 by Air World Books,
an imprint of Pen & Sword Books Ltd, Yorkshire – Philadelphia

Main Text Copyright © Flight Lieutenant D.M. Crook DFC
Introduction and Additional Text Copyright © Dilip Sarkar MBE, FRHistS

ISBN: 978 1 39900 336 0

Typeset by Mac Style
Printed and bound in the UK by CPI Group (UK) Ltd,
Croydon, CR0 4YY.

Pen & Sword Books Ltd incorporates the imprints of Pen & Sword Archaeology,
Air World Books, Atlas, Aviation, Battleground, Discovery, Family History,
History, Maritime, Military, Naval, Politics, Social History, Transport,
True Crime, Claymore Press, Frontline Books, Praetorian Press,
Seaforth Publishing and White Owl

For a complete list of Pen & Sword titles please contact:

PEN & SWORD BOOKS LTD
47 Church Street, Barnsley, South Yorkshire, S70 2AS, UK.
E-mail: enquiries@pen-and-sword.co.uk
Website: www.pen-and-sword.co.uk

Or

PEN AND SWORD BOOKS,
1950 Lawrence Roadd, Havertown, PA 19083, USA
E-mail: Uspen-and-sword@casematepublishers.com
Website: www.penandswordbooks.com

Contents

Introduction

David Moore Crook was born the eldest child of William Clifford Crook and Winifred Moore Crook in Huddersfield on 24 November 1914. A gifted scholar, 'DMC' attended The Leys School in Cambridge before entering the family firm.

DMC's father had inherited the family sporting goods manufacturing business, and, by any standards, was a wealthy man, able to fund private educations for his children, a large family home, 'Glenwood, and 'Beckwood', a substantial holiday property in the Lake District. Moreover, family holidays were often taken in Switzerland.

Whilst still a schoolboy DMC had his first taste of flight and received flying lessons. This was a privileged lifestyle – and DMC had all the necessary credentials to join the socially elite Auxiliary Air Force (AAF), which he did in 1938.

Five years previously, Adolf Hitler, leader of the Nazis, had come to power in Germany, and was now hell-bent on territorial expansion. During the mid-1930s, Germany had tested new weapons and tactics on the side of the fascist dictator Franco in the Spanish Civil War and was, slowly but surely. dismantling the restrictions imposed by the 1919 Versailles Peace Settlement.

Unprepared for war, by 1938 Britain and France pursued a policy of appeasement in the hope of avoiding another war with Germany – but after the Munich Crisis of September that year, it was clear to most that war was inevitable. Haunted by the spectre of the First World War – Europe's first head-on collision with modern warfare and death on an industrial scale – disarmament was prevalent, whilst

America pursued a policy of isolationism from events in Europe. All of this cast a shadow over everyone's lives during what Charles Loch Mowatt described as the 'Devil's Decade'.

Before 1918, Britain's military aviation had been served by the Royal Flying Corps (RFC), associated with the Army, and Royal Naval Air Service (RNAS). That year, however, the General Staff decided that there should be a new air force independent of the Army and Navy, capable of waging war against an enemy's manufacturing resources. The man chosen to oversee the creation of this junior service, the Royal Air Force (RAF), was Major General Hugh Trenchard, who became the first Chief of the Air Staff (CAS).

Trenchard envisioned that all pilots should be officers – and that all officers should be pilots. Trenchard's officers were trained at Cranwell, in Lincolnshire, which was really an extension of the public-school system – and to be eligible for a commission, the applicant had to have attended such a fee-paying school. Only 5% of the population, however, could afford to send their children to such elite schools, thus preserving the professions and commissions for the top of Britain's socio-economic pyramid in what remained a clearly delineated society.

One problem that Trenchard faced was that Cranwell was unable to generate the number of trained officer pilots the RAF required. So, the CAS did two things.

Firstly, contravening his impractical requirement that all officers should be pilots, and in the interests of creating a trained reserve, in 1921, Trenchard permitted the training of a small number of Non-Commissioned Officer (NCO) pilots. These professional airmen were expected to fly for five years before resuming their original trades, whilst eligible for recall to flying duties in the event of a national emergency. The initiative was both popular and economic, although numbers were small, with only 17.1% of pilots being NCOs by 1935.

The second initiative was even more forward-thinking. It was the introduction of the Short Service Commission. Appreciating that flying is a physically demanding activity for young men, instead of serving throughout their working lives, SSC officers were able to do so for a fixed contract of four years' active service, followed by six on the reserve list.

Another sound expedient that led to an increase in the trained reserve was the creation of the AAF in 1924. If Cranwellians were the RAF's professional officer elite, the AAF was a social elite, a *corps d'elite*. Its recruits, like DMC, were generally young men of means, many of whom already owned their own aeroplanes and flew for pleasure at weekends. Indeed, the AAF was treated by many as an exclusive gentleman's club.

By 1939, there were twenty-one AAF squadrons. It was one of these, 609 (West Riding) Squadron, that Pilot Officer David Crook, with his impeccable socio-educational credentials, joined in August 1938. The AAF was based upon the territorial principle, and were locally raised, often comprising friends and relations. Whilst this certainly helped generate a unique identity and camaraderie, when the shooting started and the casualties began this, as DMC would soon discover, very negatively affected these units' morale. Indeed, after the Battle of Britain, these squadrons became unrecognisable from their pre-war incarnations, becoming no different in terms of personnel composition to any other RAF squadron, regular or otherwise. DMC's memoir, in fact, is a powerful record of that journey, from peace into war and beyond.

Formed at Yeadon on 10 February 1936, 609 was the ninth of the AAF's squadrons. It was initially equipped with the Hawker Hind biplane light-bomber, though these were replaced in time by the Hart fighter version. In August 1939, when still a part-time squadron, 609 converted to the Spitfire.

When war and mobilisation came, 609 flew from first from Catterick, defending northern England. It then moved, first to Acklington and then to Drem, near Edinburgh, providing cover to Royal Navy bases, convoy protection patrols, practice flights and searching for unidentified aircraft on the radar screen.

The squadron's first action was fought on 29 January 1940, when a Heinkel He 111 attacking a merchant ship off the mouth of the Tay was damaged. On 27 February, Red Section shot down a He 111 which crashed into the sea.

Having completed his service flying training, Pilot Officer David Crook re-joined the squadron at Drem on 5 May. Called-up for full-time service in August 1939, just as 609 received Spitfires, DMC had not flown one of the new fighters when his training began in October. It is surprising, therefore, that he was not posted to an Operational Training Unit (OTU) for conversion to type, but returned straight to 609 Squadron. Prior to the formation of OTUs, that was how things were done, with conversion to the type of aircraft a pilot would fly operationally being undertaken on the squadron.

DMC's first Spitfire flight was on 6 May 1940, but he did not go with the squadron to Northolt on 19 May, owing to a knee injury. Subsequently, 609 Squadron participated in Operation DYNAMO without Pilot Officer Crook. At this point, its pilots, like most in Fighter Command, had little or no combat experience, and none involving the Me. 109 – which was a very different proposition to a lone German bomber. During just three days of fighting over Dunkirk, 609 lost five pilots killed: it was a rude awakening.

Flying from Warmwell in the Middle Wallop Sector of 10 Group, 609 Squadron would be heavily engaged in the Battle of Britain, fighting over the South Coast, the Channel, the West Country and the South-East. It is this period of DMC's RAF career that predominantly featured in his autobiography, *Spitfire Pilot*, which was first published by Faber and Faber in 1942. His friend, Pilot Officer Geoffrey Gaunt, was, for example, shot down in flames over London on 15 September 1940 – 'Battle of Britain Day' – prompting a reflective piece of writing by DMC concerning his friend's loss.

Ranking among the finest first-hand accounts published during the Second World War, particularly for a Battle of Britain airman, *Spitfire Pilot* rightly remains a sought-after classic – all the more so as

DMC did not survive the war. His Spitfire inexplicably crashed into the sea off the Scottish coast on 18 December 1944. A married man and father, he remains missing.

Though it was first published under wartime conditions in 1942, *Spitfire Pilot* was not heavily censored – unlike Squadron Leader Brian Lane DFC's similar first-hand account *Spitfire! The Experiences of a Fighter Pilot*, which was published the same year. DMC's book was actually based on his hand-written manuscript, which he jotted down in two Stationary Office lined notebooks, hastily scribbled between sorties, and using his pilot's flying logbook for reference.

In 1990, I traced DMC's widow, Dorothy, who enthusiastically supported the idea of re-publishing *Spitfire Pilot*. She then located bound copies of DMC's original manuscript, which she kindly passed on to me.

There are many differences between what DMC had written, and what was published in 1942. *The 'Real' Spitfire Pilot* is, therefore, his original, completely uncensored and unedited words, shared here for the first time – the book being presented in the same two volumes as the author had penned them.

It is all here within the pages of *The 'Real' Spitfire Pilot*, everything anyone would ever reasonably want to know about what it was like to be a fighter pilot that fateful summer. DMC has a knack of taking the reader with him on this epic adventure, one in which we get to know his friends and comrades – and feel their loss keenly. So, read on – and take to the air with Pilot Officer David Crook and 609 Squadron during our Finest Hour.

Dilip Sarkar MBE, FRHistS
Worcester, 2020

Acknowledgements

This book would not have been possible without the enthusiastic co-operation many years ago of David Crook's widow, the sadly now late Dorothy Hessling, and her second husband, the also late Dennis Hessling MBE.

As always, my friends Andy Long and Martin Mace provided support along the way, and the Pen & Sword team are always a pleasure to work with.

Preface

The feeling has been growing on me for some time now that I should keep a diary – or at any rate a written record of one's experiences and feelings and thoughts during these momentous last few weeks.

At the start of the war and then all through those long and rather dull winter months at Little Rissington, there seemed at the time to be very little that was worth recording. Now I realise that it would have been far better to have started this account then, because even if nothing very exciting happened, I met many interesting and some very outstanding people, and I think that one's impressions of them and the events of the early months of the war, will prove to be of some interest in later years.

But since July 1st, 1940, when I rejoined the squadron, the R.A.F. have been engaged in the biggest and fiercest battles of this or any other war. These battles reached their climax in the week starting August 8th, and the events of those long summer days may well prove to have been one of the turning points of the war for the hitherto all conquering German Air Force received its first setback.

Only a few hundred British pilots took part in these battles and as I was one of them, I feel that it would indeed be a pity not to record some of these unique experiences, which were shared by so few persons.

As this is a diary of the war, I intend starting it on Sunday, August 13th, 1939.

Flight Lieutenant D.M. Crook DFC

List of Illustrations

1. DMC (centre) and chums on a pre-war skiing holiday in Switzerland.
2. DMC, second left, and pals, pre-war skiing trip.
3. Pilot Officer David Moore Crook, Auxiliary Air Force, 1939.
4. Dorothy Middleton, whom DMC married at Lindley Parish Church, Yorkshire, on 23 August 1939. The couple would have three children: Nicholas, Rosemary and Elizabeth.
5. 'Warmwell, April 1940. Back row: Michael Appleby, Sgt Froud, "Greg". Front row: Basil Fisher, John McGrath, Self, Gordon Mitchell, F/Lt Berryman, Roger Forshaw, Bell, Jon Hay, Claude Goldsmith.'
6. A portrait of DMC.
7. Another photograph of DMC.
8. DMC at the controls of his Spitfire. The original, hand-written caption states: 'Me and my beloved Spitfire!'
9. Crook's Spitfire, PR-L, at Northolt. DMC's original caption states: 'July 1st at Northolt. Me and my Spitfire, the evening before our patrol over France.'
10. The same spot at RAF Northolt in May 2021.
11. 'Taken at Northolt, July 1st 1940: John Curchin, Michael Appleby, Pip Barran and Gordon Mitchell.'
12. Personnel of 609 Squadron in August 1940. In the front row, on the left, is DMC, whilst to the right of him is Vernon Charles 'Shorty' Keough.
13. DMC's original caption for this image states: 'Re-arming my Spitfire after the fight on July 9th. A new oxygen bottle is being put in the cockpit.'

14. '13 August 1940. Some of the Squadron just after Weymouth fight. Standing: Red, Osti, G., E., Michael, Frank, the CO, Mac, Sergeant F., Novi and Teeny. In front: Mike, DMC & Mick.'

15. A picture of 609 Squadron's duty board at Warmwell, 13 August 1940.

16. DMC's Spitfire pictured being tended by groundcrew in August 1940. His handwritten caption notes the following: 'Re-arming my Spitfire after the fight above Portland, August 13, 1940.'

17. 'Readiness, September 1940: Shorty, Geoff and DMC'. From front to back are Pilot Officer Vernon Charles 'Shorty' Keough (an American), Pilot Officer Geoffrey Gaunt and Pilot Officer David Moore Crook. One source states that Crook is seen here 'writing his wartime diary'.

18. As DMC himself stated, this image shows him 'Taking off for one of the London battles, September 1940.'

19. The wreckage of the Dornier Do.17Z, F1+FH from 1/KG76, that crashed near Victoria Station on Sunday, 15 September 1940. It had taken off from its base at Nivelles, just south of Beauvais, at 10.05 hours with 27-year-old Oberleutnant Robert Zehbe at the controls. (Historic Military Press)

20. Firemen and ARP personnel deal with the wreckage of Dornier Do.17 F1+FH in front of Victoria Station on 15 September 1940. This is an example of a 'Wirephoto', which was cabled from London to New York for immediate publication. (Historic Military Press)

21. DMC, on the left, with his great friend Pilot Officer Geoffrey Gaunt – shot down over London in flames and killed on 15 September 1940.

22. Geoffrey Gaunt's grave at Salendine Nook Baptist Chapel, Huddersfield, Yorkshire. (Glenn Gelder)

23. A still taken from the camera gun footage of DMC's Spitfire on 30 September 1940. In his memoir he wrote: 'The Me. 109 on fire and turning on his back just before diving into the sea.'

Isle of Wight on 28 November 1940, having himself shot down, seconds earlier, the German ace Major Helmut Wick.

40. DMC pictured whilst instructing on Hurricanes.

41. Another photograph of DMC taken during his time as an instructor on Hurricanes.

42. DMC the flying instructor and veteran fighter ace.

43. DMC and an unidentified fellow instructor.

44. Flight Lieutenant David Moore Crook DFC remains missing and is commemorated on the Runnymede Memorial.

45. The panel at Runnymede on which Crook is commemorated by name.

46. Three sample pages of DMC's original hand-written manuscript for *Spitfire Pilot* – and which are published here in this edition.

47. The front cover of the first edition of *Spitfire Pilot* which was published by Faber and Faber in 1942.

48. The late Dorothy Hessling, DMC's widow, photographed at home in Acocks Green, Birmingham, by Dilip Sarkar in 1990.

49. During the Battle of Britain, 609 Squadron was one of two Spitfire squadrons based at Warmwell in Dorset, inland of Weymouth. Several of the Few lie at rest there at Holy Trinity.

50. Amongst the casualties at Holy Trinity is 609 Squadron's Sergeant Alan Feary, killed in action on 7 October 1940 – one of seven pilots lost by 609 Squadron during the Battle of Britain. In DMC's book, the twenty-eight-year old reservist from Derbyshire is referred to simply as 'Sergeant F.'.

51. Pilot Officer Rogers Miller – whose fatal collision in combat with a Me. 110 DMC witnessed on 27 September 1940. Miller's story is told in Dilip Sarkar's *Battle of Britain 1940: The Finest Hour's Human Cost* (Pen & Sword, 2020).

52. The crash site near Lymington, Hampshire, of the Me. 109E-1 destroyed by Pilot Officer 'Novi' Nowierski on 15 October 1940, an incident witnessed by DMC and referred to in his manuscript. The German pilot, Obergefrieter A. Pollach of 4/JG2 baled out and was captured.

Volume I

August 1939–June 1940

We were on our last day of camp at Church Fenton, and, sitting on the steps of the Mess reading the Sunday papers on a glorious summer's morning, I really felt for the first time that war was not only probable, but that it was now inevitable.

The Danzig question was looming larger and more menacing every day, the Poles were obviously not going to give way; Germany was calling up all her reserves "for the autumn manoeuvres" and adopting a more bullying and truculent tone in every speech by one of her leaders, and England, tired of conciliatory methods which were always mistaken for weakness, and with bitter memories of Munich only twelve months before, was now determined that on this issue at any rate we would stand our ground firmly, whatever the cost.

And so, slowly at first and then with increasing speed as August went by, we appeared to be moving on towards the inevitable end.

This is not intended to be a full day to day account of my experiences since last August – many things have been forgotten that were of no importance, and almost a year has now elapsed so that it is possible to see events in their true perspective and to select those worthy of recording.

Nor do I intend to include anything very personal or private, because it is impossible then to let anybody read this account, which would be rather a pity as most of it deals with matters of general interest, such as the doings of the Squadron etc.

Therefore, I am not including anything personal about Dorothy or myself, except to say that despite the war and all its inevitable worry and anxiety, this year since our marriage has been by far the happiest year of my life.

And that is saying a very great deal since all those years have been so happy.

For our annual camp in 1939, 609 Squadron went to Church Fenton near Tadcaster. We had a very enjoyable if somewhat hard-working fortnight, and a number of us – Geoff Gaunt, Pip Barran, Gordon Mitchell, Jerry Golledge, etc spent the middle weekend – August Bank Holiday – in Scarborough.

Dorothy came over from Huddersfield and she, Geoff and I spent the weekend at the White Swan and Mrs Cooper's at Hunmanby. We met all the others in Scarborough on Friday and Saturday evening and had a very gay and hilarious weekend altogether.

I think the two most amusing episodes occurred when we got back to the White Swan late on Friday night, to find all doors locked and no reply to our knocking. Finally, I scrambled through a tiny window at the back and found myself in the maids' lavatory. However, I managed to make my way to the door and got it open. The pub keeper was most intrigued the following morning to know how we had managed to get in and simply would not believe it possible for anybody of my girth to get through such a small window.

We also had a rather exciting and amusing trip on the "Scarborough Queen" or whatever the ship is called.

The sea was very choppy and the 609-contingent insisted on standing up in the bows where we all got absolutely soaked. I shall always remember seeing Pip, clad only in a light flannel suit, standing there grinning away while the sea poured over him!

On the last Friday of camp, I took a Hind up to 16,000 feet and then flew over Huddersfield and did a few loops, upward rolls, etc., which apparently caused some stir in the place as I came fairly low.

I gathered afterwards that a lot of people stood in the streets and stared for some time – aerobatics are quite a novelty in Hudd!

I got reasonably proficient on the Hind at camp – it is a lovely aeroplane to handle and very good for aerobatics, particularly for loops. It is one of the joys of life to dive a Hind to about 230 m.p.h., open the throttle and pull her up into a vertical climb. She seems to have almost unlimited power and goes on zooming up till finally she has almost stopped and you pull the stick hard back into your tummy and go right over and dive out swiftly on the other side! Grand!

We flew back to Yeadon on Sunday afternoon August 13th (exactly a year later to the day, we were to have our most successful action of the war to date and shoot down 13 enemy machines in 5 minutes. But we could not know this at the time and in any case only three of the original 14 members of the squadrons were left with us to take part in this action).

After landing at Yeadon, I drove back home and found everybody – including Joyce who had come up to get her bridesmaid dress etc., down at Kirkfield inspecting the progress being made by the painters and decorators.

All through this week we seemed to be very busy making arrangements for the house, and the wedding, and my bachelor party in London – what a party that was to have been!

Dorothy and Joyce returned to Westgate on Sea on Friday, and we said goodbye to each other firmly expecting that we should next meet in the aisle of the church on the Great Day! What a hope!

That weekend, the family went up to Beckside and I spent the weekend with Geoff. We went over to Yeadon on the Saturday afternoon and I went up for about an hour – my last flight in peace. It was a lovely day, and I flew up over Burnsall and Skipton to Gargrave, where the annual show was in progress. I did a loop over the showground for the benefit of some of our workmen who live there and then wandered gently back to Yeadon.

The countryside was looking very lovely and very peaceful – it seemed incredible that within a fortnight we should be on the eve of war.

During the afternoon, the C.O. and Jerry Golledge had been down to Southampton to collect two Spitfires – we were very thrilled about this as we had been promised them for some time past, and now at long last we were getting them. They arrived safely back at Yeadon and dived over the aerodrome at very high speed. We were duly impressed!

That evening the C.O. invited us to dinner at the Queens in Leeds.

He dined and wined us exceedingly well, and after a distinctly cheerful party, Geoff and I returned to Glenwood, altogether taking a very rosy view of life in general!

The following morning was foggy and so we stayed in bed all morning, went up to the Nags Head for a beer before lunch and then slept all afternoon and went down to the George in the evening. The six o'clock news announced the laying of obstructions in the Firth of Forth and the Solent and I remember thinking that this was just another stage towards war.

On Monday morning we opened the newspapers to receive a very rude shock. Russia had signed a non-aggression pact with Germany and made it almost certain that the latter, with her hands free in the East, could now turn her full weight against Poland and the Western Powers. That night Geoff and I again went over to Yeadon.

The evening was misty and we did not fly. The C.O. said that he thought that war was now inevitable, and all the way back to Huddersfield I was debating in my mind whether it would be wise to leave our wedding to the date planned – September 2nd. By the time we got home I had made up my mind; we must get married as soon as possible.

As soon as I got into the house, I spoke to Mother and Father and though they were a bit staggered at first, they quite agreed and so I rang up Dorothy at Westgate. She also seemed somewhat surprised! But agreed to talk it over with her family and ring up again in the morning. She did so and told me on Tuesday that she would come up on Wednesday and get married on Thursday. I spent a little time at the works that day – my last day of civilian life – and rushed around arranging about special licences etc.

But on the Tuesday night, the news was so threatening and the Government announced that certain personnel were already being called up, that I felt there was very little time now left, and we decided to alter the date again and get married the following day – Wednesday.

Wednesday – the twenty-third day of August, nineteen hundred and thirty-nine – my (or rather, our) Wedding day!

I don't think that either of us look back on that day with much satisfaction or pleasure. It was so hurried and improvised, and always with the feeling behind it all that unless we were jolly quick, we might not manage it.

Paul and I went over to Wakefield and met the London train at about 5 p.m. They had all arrived safely and the most important person looked in very good form, though actually I believe she had the "wind up" badly!

I had been so busy all day that I had had no time to get nervous, or I should have probably been reduced to an abject state of nerves by the time of the ceremony!

Well, we got to the church safely and about 15 minutes later walked into the vestry again as man and wife.

Paul proved to be a noble best man and produced the ring promptly when required.

And so – home and a drink and a toast (while Paul and the others made such a mess of the Wolseley as I have never seen). We then departed, but had to return to drop sundry tin cans etc., and clear confetti off everything. (Three months later there was still some of the confounded stuff in my suitcase).

And so, we finally departed on our honeymoon. We stopped for dinner at Giggleswick, and then on to the Drunken Duck.

Next morning, the maid came into our room about 8 a.m. and said that I was required on the phone.

I had an awful feeling that I knew what it was and went downstairs with a sinking heart. I was quite right. It was Paul ringing up to say that five minutes after we had left the house the previous evening, the Adjutant had rung up to say that mobilisation of the Auxiliary Air Force had been ordered.

Father spoke to him and finally got permission for me to return the following day.

So that was that.

We had breakfast and departed. It was a perfect morning, the lakes were looking as lovely as I have ever seen them, and the prospect of leaving this heavenly spot which we had chosen for our honeymoon, and going back to war was too awful for words. Altogether Thursday, August 24th, 1939, ranks as one of the blackest days of my life!

We got back for lunch and found that Paul also had been called up. We both got out our uniforms, packed our kit and said goodbye.

And thus ended our easy civilian existence, and, as far as Dorothy and I were concerned, it also ended the prospect of life at Kirkfield, and the whole future which had seemed so certain only a few short weeks previously, now seemed to collapse.

When I arrived at Yeadon, I found a scene of great activity, and everybody seemed in very good spirits and in some cases very much looking forward to the future, come what may. I think that but for my wedding the previous day I should have felt the same – at any rate my very depressed spirit rose considerably, especially when I learned that there was no immediate prospect of being moved, and I could therefore live at home for the present.

There was not much to do at Yeadon – we were not yet equipped with Spitfires and were not operational and all flying was stopped.

So, we got our gas masks, and sat in the mess and drank some beer and talked, and speculated on what the immediate future might hold.

The gramophone kept going intermittently – "Roll out the Barrel" being the favourite record, I think!

On the way home that night I called in at the Drill Hall to see Paul.

There was a scene of great activity as men came in, having been called up. There was a lot of transport been loaded in the yard and everything looked as though the great moment for which they had all been training for months had now arrived at last.

Very little happened in the next few days, except that on Sunday, August 27th, the squadron moved to its war station at Catterick. About 70 men stayed on at Yeadon and in addition the following officers stayed behind as we were not fully trained – Self, Gordon Mitchell, Michael Appleby, Geoffrey Gaunt, Patrick Womersley and the Accountant Officer – Tony Fletcher and the Adjutant, Dodgshun (he later went to a Bomber Squadron and is now a prisoner of war).

All through the week Sir Neville Henderson was making his last efforts for a settlement; the Navy and then the Army were mobilised, traffic lights started to be covered up save for a tiny slit, pavements and curbs were painted white and everywhere people started thinking how to blackout their houses.

On the Wednesday, Dorothy came over to Yeadon and I took her up in a club Moth in the afternoon.

We flew over Paul's searchlight position and wandered round Otley and the Chevin.

I think D. quite enjoyed it – her first flight incidentally – but steep turns did not appeal to her!

On the Friday morning I walked into Headquarters at about 9.30 a.m. and heard the C.O. telling somebody that the Germans had invaded Poland at dawn that morning.

This was final – it was now only a question of hours before we also were at war with Germany. I walked over to the Link Trainer and told Geoff and Gordon and Michael who were all there. I remember that Gordon was "under the hood" in the machine when I went in and when we told him the news, he appeared to think that we were to pulling his leg.

John Fletcher, the Assistant Adjutant and my instructor left that day on being posted to Cranwell. I was very sorry to see him go – he was a jolly good chap as well as a most patient and long-suffering instructor!

From that night onwards all lights were to be dimmed on cars and no light could be shown from houses.

The blackout seemed very strange at first – almost as strange as it would be now to see everything lit up again.

On Sunday, September 3rd, I went over to Yeadon in good time. It had been announced that our ultimatum to Germany to stop her invasion of Poland was to expire at 11 a.m.

I happened to be orderly officer that day and about 10.30 a.m. some very trivial message had to be a deciphered. I went into the C.O.'s office, took out the codes, and started to work. I finished just before 11 a.m., and sat, and waited, and thought. The fatal hour came and a moment later I locked up the codes, and walked out with a curious but rather exciting feeling. We were at war!

I went over to the Mess and had a beer with the others, and listened to Chamberlain's speech.

Thus started the war at Yeadon!

For a month after the declaration of war our life at Yeadon was enjoyable but uneventful.

We used to listen to the news bulletins, and scan the papers eagerly for startling news, but there was nothing very sensational, just the steady over-running of Poland, despite her gallant resistance against overwhelming odds. There was the R.A.F. raid at Kiel, which seemed such an event at the time, but now would be regarded as merely an incident in a day's fighting, along with the leaflet raids which were so criticised but later proved to have given our bomber crews such excellent knowledge of night raids into Germany.

I think that everybody in this country expected that from the word "Go" the German Air Force would come over in hundreds and literary plaster the country with high explosives. For years the might of the German Air Force had been discussed in the newspapers and to almost everybody it appeared likely that we should get our first raids very shortly.

I slept at Yeadon that night in the H.Q. offices, and about 2.30 a.m., one of the guard came in and said that the sirens were going. I leapt out of bed – sure enough, all the sirens for many miles around were wailing.

There it was at last!

I was distinctly nervous – these affairs are so much worse when you are wakened suddenly in the night!

I walked outside. It was a lovely starlit night and everything was absolutely still. Somewhat reassured I went back and a few minutes later the All Clear went. It had all been a mistake!

I find it rather amusing to compare our panic then with the calmness and even slight amusement with which we greet real raids in these days – unless they come too close.

For the rest of September, I continued to live at home, and as discipline gradually relaxed and things got slacker, I sometimes used to arrive at Yeadon at 11.30 a.m. and have lunch and a sleep and go back at 4 p.m.

There was no flying, but we used to spend some time every day in the Link Trainer and were quite good at blind flying at the end of our time.

For the rest we played rugger once or twice a week and also played mixed hockey with the W.A.A.F.s.

These were amusing but not very skilful as the W.A.A.F.s were generally chosen for their decorative rather than their athletic qualifications. The two did not seem to combine very well on the whole but we enjoyed the hockey all the same!

Talking of W.A.A.F.s, two very amusing orders came out at the beginning of the war – both issued by the Air Ministry. These are quite true:

"If any member of the W.A.A.F.s is discovered to be pregnant, headquarters will be informed and further instructions will be sent through later".

"If any member of the W.A.A.F. is discovered to be suffering from V.D. she will be required to resign at once as His Majesty has no further use for her services".

Also, on the question of leave passes and the forms which were issued on the subject, "W.A.A.F. personnel will show their pink forms when required on leave".

For the remainder of the month, we continued to play rugger, and have some very hilarious parties both at the Prospect in Harrogate and also at the Peacock at Yeadon.

I rode my motorbike over every day and altogether life was very pleasant, though we sometimes used to grumble about it being "dull".

Little did we realise that this month was probably the easiest and altogether the most enjoyable that we should ever have during the war.

On Sunday, October 1st, D. and I made up our minds that as we had not had a honeymoon, we would jolly well have a couple of days now. Accordingly, we went up to the Red Lion at Burnsall, and had two very happy days in glorious autumn weather. The river and the trees were as lovely as ever and we walked, and played darts in the bar, and drank a little beer and went to the service on Sunday evening. The Curate was not very inspiring, but it was a beautiful little church, and I shall always remember that evening.

A few days before, we had got permission to fly again, and so Michael came over to Burnsall by arrangement and entertained us with a few loops etc., to the intense gratification of the small boys (and indeed everybody) in the village. I don't think they were very good loops, but still!

On Tuesday we left Burnsall and returned to Yeadon, where I had a very enjoyable hour of aerobatics in a Tutor. I hadn't flown for some time and my first slow roll was perhaps the most astonishing contortion that any aeroplane ever performed.

On Saturday, October 7th, we were due to play Leeds Y.M.C.A. at rugger in the afternoon and Geoff, Dorothy and I were sitting in the Peacock having our beer before lunch when Dodgshun, the Adjutant, rang me up and said that orders had just come through for Patrick Womersley and me to go to No.6 Flying Training School at Little Rissington in Gloucestershire. We had been expecting this move, but it wasn't very welcome when it came. I realised that life now wasn't going to be quite the easy existence it had been so far, and though the idea of serious flying was very welcome, I thought I might see very little of D. in the future.

Anyway, we finished our beer, went back to Yeadon and had lunch and a bottle of champagne to drink a toast to the future. I packed my flying kit said goodbye to everybody, and D. and I drove off.

As far as I was concerned this ended the first and probably the most enjoyable phase of the war.

Certainly, I never had a gayer time in my life – or so it seems now when looking back. The war was very quiet and if any of us did wonder at times what might be our fate in the future, such reflections were soon lost in the presence of such gay and lively companions.

All my life, I have often been reminded of events or people by some tune which I associated with them and on hearing this tune later, even after a period of years, the same flood of memories always comes back to me.

In the future, whenever I hear "Roll out the Barrel", or "Wishing", or "Transatlantic Lullaby", I shall think of Yeadon in September 1939.

After two days at Little Rissington I felt like a pricked balloon – very flat and disillusioned.

The Auxiliary Air Force always considered themselves rather a thing apart from the R.A.F. both as regards discipline and a number of other matters.

Nobody had ever tried to suggest to us that this was not the case, and when about 9 Auxiliary Officers arrived at Rissington on the first wartime course and discovered that we were expected to conform with regular R.A.F. standards of discipline, we felt very bitter about it.

Actually, it was an excellent lesson for our rather conceited selves – I can see that now but rather failed to perceive it then! Certainly, some of the rules were designed to meet the case of boys of 18-20 years old, straight from school, and the "men of the world" aged 25 or so, found these rather childish and said so.

But on the whole, we had the good sense to lie low for a while and not make a nuisance of ourselves. I think that Peter Dunning White was the only real exception in this case.

Whereas most of us resolved from the outset that we would not be treated like the rest, we also realised that we should have to prepare the way with some care.

Peter, however, took a thoroughly uncompromising attitude from the very beginning and I must say I rather admired him for it.

He started on the first day by arriving in a Rolls coupe (cars being forbidden to first term pupils), and asking one of the instructors where the garages were.

Again, on our third morning there, the whole course were paraded and drilled by Warrant Officer Marsh, a man of fearsome aspect who had been in the Indian Army for 25 years. He told us exactly what he thought of us, our appearance and general smartness and finally told us to get our hair cut before we came on parade again. We were all very indignant – being told to have a haircut by an N.C.O. – unheard of!

We certainly weren't going etc., etc., etc. However, everybody turned up next morning all shaved and shorn – except Peter. I think that the news of this and other incidents reached the ears of Ellis, the Station C.O. because he always had a soft spot for Peter after that.

However, we soon found life more bearable, and by working hard and doing better than any previous course at the school we created a good impression and finally the authorities became far more human and friendly in attitude.

About two days after Patrick and I arrived, I was surprised to see Michael in the mess one evening – he had not been posted at the same time as us and I thought that our ways had parted. Also, Gordon came back from hospital, where he had been for a few weeks and so we had some of the old crowd together again. I was very pleased about this.

For the first two months at Rissington we definitely worked very hard indeed, both at flying and ground work.

Lectures or parade started at 7.45 a.m. and after that we flew all morning and had lectures all afternoon and, on alternate days, lectures in the morning and flying in the afternoon.

I enjoyed the flying and did not have any difficulty with this, but the lectures were not so enjoyable.

To have to sit at a desk with books in front of you and see an instructor explaining a navigational problem on the blackboard is far too like algebra lessons at school for my liking. But I think that we all realised that this might prove very useful and even essential to us one day in the not too distant future, and so we worked hard and didn't go to sleep and waded through engines and supercharging, airframes and rigging, guns and armaments, meteorology and navigation, till we all possessed a fairly good idea of the subjects.

At Flying Training School, the Chief Ground Instructor (C.G.I.) is really the equivalent of a housemaster at public school – he watches your progress, punishes you if lazy, gives you leave or stops your leave as you deserve and altogether keeps you up to scratch.

We had a very good C.G.I. at Rissington – Scragg by name who was a Flying Officer acting Squadron Leader.

He was a jolly good chap with a strong personality, and after a somewhat austere welcome, we all got on very well with him. He was "a beast, but a just beast" and if you went to him with a good case, he was always reasonable. But he could be merciless!

In his more humorous moments (such as Guest Nights) he used to refer to himself as "the old bastard".

He was up in his office one day when he heard somebody outside say to somebody else, "is the old bastard in?" This delighted Scragg!

Soon after we arrived at Rissington a very amusing episode occurred concerning a rather odd and erratic pupil called Maritz, who was a South African Boer, and the most irresponsible individual that I have ever met. He regarded a cheque book as a heaven-sent method of paying for anything, and the fact that his cheques were almost always returned R.D. (refer to drawer) never worried him. When the authorities heard of this, they threw him out, but one evening before this happened Maritz was seen by an instructor from Rissington sitting in his greatcoat in a London bar.

I enjoyed the flying at Rissington very much, and soon got to like the Harvard. This machine is one of the types that we are getting from America, and I must say that it gave me a very good impression of American aircraft. It is very well built, easy to maintain, and has a marvellous engine – the Pratt and Witney Wasp.

I don't think we ever had a case of engine failure the whole seven months that we were at Rissington.

The Harvard is not very fast – its maximum speed is about 180 m.p.h. but it cruises along very comfortably at 150 m.p.h. and is a delightful machine for aerobatics. At first it had a rather bad reputation in the R.A.F. because quite a number of fatal crashes occurred – some of them involving very experienced pilots. Certainly, the Harvard does require handling with care, and possesses a very vicious spin, especially to the right. But if you treat them with a little respect, then they are very pleasant machines and certainly we all became very devoted to them.

I remember that I was rather impressed by my first spin in a Harvard.

At about 6,000 feet, I throttled back and when she had almost stalled, I put on right rudder. The machine promptly executed a fearsome leap over to the right, and started to spin down very rapidly. I didn't wait very long before recovering – I put on full left rudder and pushed the control column forward to the dashboard. She stopped spinning almost immediately, but I had the stick too far forward and the result was that we came out in a dive beyond the vertical. We lost at least 3,000 feet before pulling up, and I had considerable respect for a Harvard spin after that!

My flying instructor was a little chap called Newton-Howes – he later went out to Australia as flying instructor.

He was very short, and – to put it mildly – not very good looking, and altogether I was rather appalled at first. But he improved a lot as I got to know him better, and if he wasn't a particularly brilliant pilot, he was very sound, and possessed the essential qualification for instructing – he was very patient. I think he regarded me as one of his best pupils – he always took particular interest in my flying and altogether we got on very well.

Our Flight Commander was "Paddy" Cole – a grand Irishman who was one of the best people we met at Rissington. He was a jolly good pilot and altogether a distinct character – we were all very fond of him.

We also had an excellent Chief Flying Instructor – Squadron Leader Oliver. He had spent a lot of time on flying boats out in Singapore and had met Gordon Mitchell out there. He was a grand person, very powerfully built and with a striking face that might have been very good looking but for a somewhat battered nose – the result of a lot of boxing. He had a terrific personality and if he made us work hard, at any rate, he got the best out of us.

Not long after we left Rissington he got married, and shortly after he went to command a Hurricane squadron. He was killed in action during the fighting in August.

We were very shocked to hear of his death, he always seemed so alive and tough that it was difficult to imagine him dying.

My main concern when we got to Rissington was to find out whether or not it was possible for pupils to live out with their wives.

I soon discovered a fellow conspirator in this – Bunny Gordon, who possessed a very amusing and delightful American wife, Louise.

He lived in Aberdeen, but was determined not to leave Louise there all winter as she had not been there long and knew very few people, and would have been very lonely. Also, she had lived all her life in California and the thought of wintering in the North of Scotland appalled her!

So, Bunny and I decided to see what could be done.

It seemed hopeless at first – it had never been allowed before and was absolutely against rules, but by approaching the matter carefully and also suggesting very delicately that we were Auxiliary Air Force officers, and therefore expected different treatment, we finally obtained permission.

So, a week after our arrival, on Saturday, October 14th, (the day after the *Royal Oak* was torpedoed in Scapa Flow), Dorothy came down to Bourton-on-the-Water and we went to live at the New Inn, which was to be our home for seven long months.

Bourton is a very picturesque village in the heart of the Cotswolds, and there is a very pretty stream – the Windrush – which runs right through the village, through gardens, past the village green, and under a number of little footbridges. During the summer, crowds of trippers and charabancs – mainly from Birmingham – descend on the place at weekends and rather spoil it. But fortunately, we were there during the winter so were not troubled by crowds. The New Inn is a typical small English country pub and is pleasant enough for a short stay, but we got very tired of it after a few months. This applied particularly to Dorothy as she had to spend all her time there, whereas I was up at the aerodrome most of the day.

But on the whole, we were very comfortable there and the Morris's, who owned the place, were always very friendly and obliging.

I had my motorbike sent down from home and for the first few months there I used to drive up the long hill to Rissington at 6.30 a.m. every morning. The weather was often appalling and the motor bike being somewhat ancient, I sometimes had to walk a good way up the hill after it had "passed out" with some mysterious ignition trouble. Altogether, I was very glad on my first leave at home in December to get the Wolseley down, and life was much easier after this. How well I know that road up from Bourton to the aerodrome! The first mile runs along the valley by the Windrush and after that turns over a bridge and then starts to climb for the first part of the hill up to the tiny village of Little Rissington. Past the village, the hill becomes steeper and goes round a sharp corner and then tops the brow of the ridge and you go straight on to the crossroads and turn right for the aerodrome.

On October 27th, I flew to Peterborough in the afternoon on a cross country flight, and then caught the 5.10 p.m. train from Kingham to Paddington and met D. in London – she had gone up a day or two before and had been staying in Walmer.

We had a very pleasant weekend and saw the Palladium show "The Little Dog Laughed" which produced what was probably the best tune of the early months of the war – "Franklin D. Roosevelt Jones".

I think that is the song which will always remind me of the first winter of war.

We had several more weekends in town while at Rissington, and generally spent them with Michael and Gordon.

I think the most memorable weekend was on Friday, November 24th, which we regard as our "celebration" as my birthday is on November 24th, Dorothy's is on the 26th, and our first meeting took place on the 28th.

Obviously, this had to be celebrated. So, Dorothy, Michael, Gordon and myself, went up to town and there met Geoff who had come up from Reading, where he was at an Elementary Flying Training School. We saw "Black Velvet" at the Hippodrome, and then had a distinctly hilarious dinner at the Troc, where we met Hugh Johnson and his girlfriend, and went on to the Paradise where we danced till the very small hours before adjourning to Lyons for bacon and eggs. We never went to bed at all.

We returned to Rissington to face a week of very hard work before our "wings" exam. We all viewed our prospects with some misgivings, but it was all right on the day and we all passed. Rarely have I felt such satisfaction as when D., sewed that coveted distinction on my tunic. We were now real pilots!

On looking back now, I think we all realised that we still didn't know very much about service flying – at any rate, not compared with what we have learnt since – but we felt very important at the time!

As the weather got worse, the aerodrome became more and more muddy, till finally all flying at Rissington was stopped.

This meant that life became very dull, and I think that a lot of people's drink bills in the mess mounted very rapidly.

We used to have some very cheery evenings down at the New Inn, and often Michael, Gordon, John McGrath and Julian Smithers came down and had dinner with us and stayed afterwards in the little bar which filled up more and more as the evening progressed, till finally you could scarcely move, and the atmosphere was so thick with smoke it looked like a fog.

And so, life continued through the winter. Barbara and Bill came to stay at the New Inn for a week after they were married, and then moved over to March Haddon Farm at Brize Norton. We could not see very much of them owing to petrol shortage, but we spent one or two weekends with them, and went over to dances in the mess there, which were always very good fun, particularly when Paul and Kath came to one in March, and Gordon Mitchell also happened to be there, so we passed a very enjoyable evening.

Paul and Katherine were married at Brenley on December 9th and the whole family assembled there for the event. The service was a delightful one, and afterwards we all went into Canterbury for an excellent dinner. Altogether a great contrast with our own hurried marriage!

We all got a week's leave for Xmas, and so Dorothy and I went up to Huddersfield and on the following day we all – including Barbara and Bill – went up to Beckside.

Unfortunately, Paul and Kath could not come up as Paul could not get leave.

We had not been up there since our ill-fated honeymoon and everything seemed exactly the same – just as peaceful and lovely as ever. We all did quite a lot of walking and did the usual Xmas day walk over Latterbarrow and down to Belle Grange. Dorothy and I went up to the Duck, where John Harrison-Broadley stood us the bottle of champagne he had promised us for our honeymoon, but which we had never claimed. It tasted just as good after four months waiting!

Altogether a marvellous weekend – it was grand to be all together up there again.

When we returned to Rissington after Xmas, the weather was still hopeless, but towards the end of January it improved and we started flying over at Kidlington aerodrome, just north of Oxford.

Rissington was still a sea of mud. We were now in the Advanced Training Squadron and the flying was very good fun. We used to work quite a lot in pairs (my partner being Gordon) and went off on navigation or reconnaissance exercises over quite a large area of Southern England. Sometimes two or three of us would meet at some pre-arranged rendezvous and then go low flying all over the high ground above Bourton, sweeping in line over farms and houses, and on one famous occasion making a man in a field throw himself flat on his face! We used to roar down the roads just over charabancs and cars and then climbing up again, go back to Kidlington, rolling and diving and generally playing the fool all the way back.

Yes – those were very happy days, and we were all very happy and light-hearted and carefree. Flying seemed to be the only thing in the world that really mattered and we were all so interested and absorbed in it that it seemed to dominate our whole conversation and outlook and lives.

I possess now a very great admiration for the flying training given to pilots by the R.A.F. I don't think there is any training system in the world to touch it for thoroughness, and it also seems to impart to many of the pupils those qualities of initiative and dash which we seem to produce to our great advantage over the German Air Force, who are not half such good individualists. Certainly, when we left Rissington to take our own parts in the war, we possessed a very sound background of flying knowledge and experience, even though we still had a great deal to learn.

On April 4th, we had finished our flying and had also done our requisite number of hours night flying, so we got a few days' leave before going to Warmwell (near Weymouth) to do our firing at the Armament School there.

Dorothy and I accordingly drove up home and spent a very pleasant weekend there. I remember that a number of us went over to dance at the Majestic in Harrogate on the Saturday evening.

I drove back to Rissington on Sunday afternoon and on Monday the whole of the Fighter Flight departed for Warmwell.

This proved to be a grand ending to our course, the weather was good on the whole, we did a lot of flying and firing and had some very good evenings in Weymouth.

D. came down for the middle weekend and we had two very pleasant days at the Gloucester Hotel.

We returned to Rissington having had a grand fortnight which left some very happy recollections of Warmwell (some people returned with some distinctly romantic recollections also!).

Little did we think that some of us would again fly from Warmwell in the near future, in far grimmer and more serious circumstances.

Our time at Rissington was now almost over, and little remained to be done except to pack our kit, bid everybody farewell and – almost more important than anything else – hear what squadrons we were posted to. All the Auxiliary Officers had applied to return to their old squadrons, but we were rather anxious about this and thought that we might be posted to some unspeakable job, such as Army Co-operation or day bombers. But when the postings came through, they pleased almost everybody, and Michael, Gordon and I were all returned to 609, to our intense relief.

Our last night at Rissington was a very gay one, and (as Winston Churchill once put it) the use of alcohol was not excluded. The Group Captain, who was in fighting form, made a long speech and assured us that we should all teach "that damned Austrian house painter" a good lesson.

He also paid our course – No. 15 Course – several compliments which I think were quite well deserved, as we were undoubtedly the best course that had ever been through Rissington – all our results and particularly the air firing results were easily the best ever obtained.

I achieved one ambition by getting "Exceptional" as my flying assessment, and my confidential report said "An exceptional pilot in every way who should be a credit to any squadron" so I felt that I could look back on my time at Rissington with some satisfaction.

I hated the thought of saying goodbye to everybody. There were 15 officers on our course, and we had spent the whole winter together and got to know each other very well indeed. With all the monotony and boredom that we had to put up with sometimes, quite a lot of friction and bad temper might have been expected. But it never materialised, and one could not have wished for pleasanter or more friendly company.

I think they were easily the most charming and distinguished lot of people that I have ever met.

There were several South Africans, who had been in the Cambridge or London University Air Squadrons – Claude Goldsmith and Ian Hay were two of them, and were in the Fighter Flight, while the third, Hugh Haswell, was in the Bomber Flight, and later went to a Blenheim Squadron and was posted Missing in August. Ian Hay went to 610 Fighter Squadron, while poor old Claude, who had set his heart on getting to a Fighter Squadron also, was sent to Army Co-operation instead. I felt very sorry for him – he would have made a jolly good fighter pilot. We tried to get him and "Greg" (who was in the same flight) transferred to 609, but it could not be done.

Then there was Basil Fisher – very quiet, and with a rather shy but charming manner. He was a marvellous squash player, and an ex-Eton cricket captain.

He was simply delighted when he was posted to 111 Squadron – like the rest of us he had set his heart on getting into a fighter squadron.

He was killed in August in one of the battles off the South East coast.

John McGrath and Julian Smithers were both in 601 Squadron, and we saw a lot of them at Rissington as they often used to come down to the New Inn with Gordon and Michael.

John was an exceptionally good pilot and I don't think any of us were surprised when he got the D.F.C. in August.

Julian was killed in August, within a day or two of his fellow Etonian, Basil.

So much more could be written about them all, and the times that we used to have together, but it would take too long.

So Dorothy and I said goodbye to everybody and on Saturday, April 27th, we left Rissington and drove up home on a week's leave before joining the squadron.

It was grand to be home again and we spent a very pleasant week.

On the Wednesday we went over to Yeadon and met Michael there. It seemed very funny to go back – I had not been there since October.

Michael and I each took a Magister up for a short trip.

I wandered all round the familiar countryside – Otley, Ilkley, Burnsall, Gargrave and Skipton. It seemed just like an ordinary Saturday afternoon's flying in peace time!

When I got back, I found that Michael's engine had failed, and he had made a not too successful forced landing in a field near Otley. He turned up about half an hour later with a large bruise on his head and not at all pleased!

We really had no business to have flown the Magisters at all, and we rather wondered if there would be some trouble about the crash. But nobody seems to bother much about aeroplane crashes in war and nothing happened.

On the Friday the weather was beautiful and Dorothy and I lay on the lawn at home all afternoon and enjoyed to the full our last day of leisure.

On the Saturday morning, May 4th, I said goodbye at home and drove off – for the first time – on active service.

I had arranged to go up to Drem with Michael and Gordon, and so we met at the Queens in Leeds and had lunch with Pip Barran, who was down on leave.

Gordon stayed on in Leeds during the afternoon to see somebody, but Michael and I left in the Wolseley after lunch, and started on our long drive North.

It was a lovely day and we had a very pleasant journey – Harrogate, Ripon, and up the Great North Road to Newcastle and Alnwick, where we stopped for a drink and some sandwiches at the White Swan or whatever the pub is.

I remember pulling the car up, and looking at the view of the river from the bridge just below the castle.

On again through Berwick on Tweed, up to Haddington where we turned off to the right, climbed up over the hill and saw Drem lying down on the other side, with the Forth and the Bass Rock beyond.

It was good to be back with the squadron again after such a long absence.

They had had a very quiet and on the whole dull winter and had only been in action once, when a solitary Heinkel was shot down by Dizzy Ayre, after it had tried to attack a convoy.

We had suffered no losses at all since the outbreak of war, and everybody was in very good form and enjoying life at Drem to the utmost.

Certainly, it was a very pleasant spot. There was plenty of golf and squash and tennis – the war was very quiet and hardly entered into anybody's mind at all, and we could go into Edinburgh on most evenings. Altogether it was a very pleasant and easy existence.

The next day we did our first flight in a Spitfire. I liked the machine very much on my first trip, and since then have grown to like it far more than any other aeroplane I have flown. It is so small and compact and easy to handle, that one sometimes seems to forget its enormous power, and the very high speeds of which it is capable. It is still the fastest and probably the best fighter in the world, and though new and even faster types will shortly be coming into service, they will have to do very well to equal the Spitfire's record of success.

I thoroughly enjoyed my first week at Drem and came to the conclusion that if this was the life of the average fighter pilot in war then I didn't mind how long the war continued.

I played some squash with Gordon and Michael and, as usual, was beaten by the former and beat the latter. Michael will be very indignant when he reads this!

We also did one or two hours of flying practice every day and soon became quite at home in the Spitfire. The weather was glorious, and we used to get superb views in all directions – particularly across the Firth of Forth to the mountains in the north.

On Thursday evening, May 9th, we had the day off and so Gordon, Michael and I went into Edinburgh and had a grand evening – dinner and then on to a very amusing variety show at the Empire. The house was packed with a very noisy and appreciative audience and there was an amusing episode when a drunken sailor climbed up on to the front of the stage and tried to dance. He was cheered wildly, and then the side curtains were quickly drawn across and exactly three seconds later when they were drawn back again, the sailor had been spirited away! We all cheered more than ever! It was a marvellous evening. It was also the last evening out together that Michael, Gordon and I were to have.

The following morning about 7.30 a.m., my batman Sinclair came in and woke me with the words "Jerry's into Holland and Belgium". I bounded out of bed – this was astonishing news.

Everybody else seemed to be equally staggered, but behind the surprise I think that there was a very general sense of relief that the war had now really "started" and that as a result we might soon see some real action.

Also, the only large-scale operations that we had conducted against the Germans had been the ill-fated Norwegian campaign where we had faced such difficulties and disadvantages both on land and in the air. But this – this was different!

This was an attack almost on our own doorstep, on places where we had large armies in prepared positions, and could send reinforcements on the largest scale to any threatened point. Also, for the first time, the full weight of the R.A.F. can be brought to bear.

Now we can really give the Huns a taste of their own medicine!

Thus, we thought in our ignorance and complacency.

The new offensive, however, did not immediately disturb our easy way of life at Drem, and indeed, I think the only result was that we cancelled a cocktail party which was to have been held the following Friday. There was no bombing and no enemy activity.

This weekend being Whitsuntide, the family were up in the Lakes and I arranged with Dorothy that she should come up on the Tuesday. I went over to Edinburgh to meet her and we returned to Gullane where I had booked a room at a hotel. This was too expensive and so we found some very pleasant and inexpensive rooms in a cottage just opposite the police station that were kept by a typical Scots woman.

I think we should have been very happy there but as events turned out, we did not go.

I had the day off on Wednesday, and so D. and I went into North Berwick and walked on to the beach at Gullane, and passed a very pleasant day.

On Thursday morning, May 16th, I jumped out of bed and in doing so I tore the cartilage of my left knee – it had given me trouble for years. It was very painful and I could not move it, so D. rang up the aerodrome and they sent the ambulance to collect me. When the doctor saw it, he gave me chloroform and managed to straighten the knee, but it was still hopeless. So, the next day I went to Edinburgh to see a military doctor and he, without hesitation, sent me down to the 23rd Scottish General Hospital at Peebles Hydro for an operation.

So, a few hours later I was being carried up the steps of the Hydro on a stretcher. I was put into room 74 – a very pleasant room in the corner of the building. This was to be my home for over a month – and a very happy month it was. Peebles is a lovely place and the view from the Hydro is superb. Also, the weather was good and we spent a lot of time out on the front balcony on the top floor.

The nurses, after being rather strict at the beginning, became very friendly and they were always extremely efficient and helpful, while the Sister was a grand person – a typical dry, kindly Scots woman.

Also, there were some very amusing and entertaining fellow patients – Moss, who was in the Fleet Air Arm; Monk, in the R.A.F.; Major Fraser in the Gordons; and Duff, who was a Scottish rugger international, and looked like a great amiable guerrilla lying in bed.

Major Muir, my doctor, proved to be a very pleasant fellow and after X-raying my knee it was decided to operate on the following Wednesday.

To my surprise Dorothy turned up on the day after my arrival there. I hadn't expected her for a day or two, but she came down in the car with Elaine Sudworth. They also brought the news that the squadron had been ordered south to Northolt.

D. found some very nice rooms in Peebles, first at the Waverley Hotel and then across the road with Mrs. Melrose.

She used to come up and sit with us on the balcony all day in the sun and altogether we spent a grand month, even though the news from France got worse every day. But all these disasters did not move Peebles and it remained as sleepy, as peaceful and as beautiful as ever.

My operation was about as pleasant as these affairs generally are, and I was gloriously sick afterwards! D. performed nobly with a basin, I remember!

While we were having such an easy and pleasant life, 609 were going into action for the first time at Dunkirk and also having our first losses.

On May 30th, 31st and June 1st, the squadron did patrols over Dunkirk to cover the evacuation of troops from the beaches.

We shot a number of Huns down, and lost Persse-Joynt, Dawson, Gilbert, and Russell. Desmond Ayre was also killed near Frinton on Sea – he lost his way back in bad weather and ran out of petrol, and was killed in trying to make a forced landing.

"Presser" was an Irishman – a grand fellow and "A" Flight Commander.

Russell had been attached to 609 for a few months only, and during most of the fighting in France in May he was serving in a Hurricane squadron and re-joined 609 just before Dunkirk.

He was certainly one of the best fighter pilots in the R.A.F. – he shot down 14 Germans in a fortnight and damaged a number more. He got the D.F.C. a few days before his death.

I think there is no doubt that some of these losses were due to inexperience and lack of caution. None of them, except Russell, had ever been in action before and everybody's idea was to go all out for the first Hun that appeared.

This policy does not pay when you are fighting a cunning and crafty foe, and the Germans frequently used to send over a decoy aircraft with a number of fighters hovering in the sun some thousands of feet above, which used to come down like a ton of bricks on anybody attacking the decoy. This ruse almost certainly accounted for Presser and possibly one or two others. The last that anybody saw of Presser was when he was diving down to attack a Junkers 88, and there were definitely some Messerschmitts above.

My knee was now improving rapidly and on Sunday, June 16th, D. and I left Peebles with many regrets. I shall always have some very pleasant recollections of our time there.

We arrived at home to find very considerable activity going on, as Barbara and Bill were leaving for South Africa in a few days' time.

On Monday lunchtime, the news of the French capitulation came through and everybody seemed absolutely stunned by the disaster.

On Tuesday morning Barbara and Mother and Father departed for London, on their way down to the boat at Southampton.

Having seen them off, D. and I set off for the Lakes and went to stay at Milners in Hawkshead. The weather was perfect and it was marvellous to be up there again. Joyce arrived the following day, and we all spent a very happy week together, sailing and fishing with John Harrison Broadley. On the Saturday, we moved up to the Drunken Duck and spent the rest of the week there. We regarded this almost as being a continuation of our honeymoon!

We returned home and spent two days there and on Saturday, June 29th, we departed for London and I said goodbye to D. at Marylebone and went out to Northolt, to start the most exciting and eventful time of my life.

A great change had come over the squadron since I had left them at Drem only seven weeks before. We had a new and far better C.O. and there were several new pilots to replace the Dunkirk losses.

The old easy-going outlook on life had vanished, and everybody now seemed to realise that war was not the fairly pleasant affair that it had always seemed at Drem. Altogether the general mood now appeared to be one of rather grim determination.

Northolt – like all other R.A.F. stations – had been transformed since the invasion of the Low Countries, and was now stiff with troops and barbed wire and concrete machine-gun posts, etc. I certainly could not see how it would be possible to surprise the aerodrome by a sudden landing of parachutists – they would have been simply massacred.

My first two days at Northolt were spent mainly in practice flying and attacks, and I soon felt quite at home in the Spitfire again.

July 1940

O n the Monday evening, July 1st, I came down into the anteroom and found Pip gathering everybody together as an order had just come through that 12 of us were to do a reconnaissance of some aerodromes in Northern France the following morning, in order to see what machines the enemy were assembling there. If our patrols reported a good concentration at any aerodrome, then bombers were dispatched immediately to beat the place up.

I don't think any of us were pleased about this job – very much the reverse. Quite frankly I loathed the idea! It seemed incredible that a few machines would be able to fly 30 or 40 miles into enemy territory in broad daylight, at a height of only 6,000 feet (we could not inspect the ground carefully from a greater height) and get away without serious interference from both A.A. fire and vastly superior numbers of enemy fighters. And then – a dogfight and possibly a bullet in the engine or radiator, a forced landing and prisoner for the duration. No, I was not enthusiastic!

Anyway, it had to be done, so we got out maps and discussed the route – down to Hawkinge (Folkestone) at dawn to refuel and get breakfast, then straight over to Boulogne, along the coast to the mouth of the Somme, turn in to Abbeville, and then south west again along to Rouen, where we should turn north and cross the coast at Dieppe on our way home. We reckoned that we should get to Abbeville easily but that we might expect a lot of trouble any time after that.

And so, to bed, to get what sleep we could. I gathered afterwards that nobody slept well and I certainly didn't. I had never even seen the enemy before, let alone been fired at, and I kept wondering what it would be like to go into action for the first time.

We got up about 3.30 a.m. It was a lovely morning and we got into cars and went down to the dispersal point, where our machines were already being run up. I checked everything in the cockpit particularly carefully, and a few minutes later we took off and headed south east, down through Kent to Folkestone. It was the first time that I had flown with the whole squadron and it was certainly a rather inspiring sight to see eleven other Spitfires all thundering on together.

We landed at Hawkinge and the ground crews immediately started to refuel the aircraft. We all stood around and smoked cigarettes incessantly, and made some rather forced conversation, and suffered from the that unpleasant empty feeling in the tummy that one always experiences at such moments.

Altogether a very good specimen of squadron "wind-up"!

So many reflections and recollections come back to me at such moments.

I thought of a summer's evening two years before, when Glen Pallot had been at camp here, and I had come down to see him. How different it had all seemed then!

I thought of those grand July weekends that we had spent at Brenley only a few miles away, and most of all, I thought of those occasions when we had sailed from Folkestone en route for Boulogne and Switzerland. I had a feeling that I wasn't going to enjoy this cross-channel trip quite as well as those previous ones!

The machines were now refuelled and we climbed in, started the engines and taxied out to take off. A few moments later we were in the air – one circuit of Folkestone and then we headed straight out for the French Coast. But an anti-climax was in store for us. As we approached France, we could see a ground mist covering the countryside, and the ground itself was invisible. This was no good and so we turned about and returned to Hawkinge with our task still unexecuted.

We spent an unpleasant day at Hawkinge, and although somebody went over to have a look at the weather at lunchtime, it was still no good.

During the afternoon, instructions came through that one machine was to go over at 6 p.m. and if the weather was suitable, we would take off at 7 p.m. Our scout returned at about 6.45 p.m. with the news that the weather was now okay. The time had arrived! I really didn't care very much any longer – after waiting all day. I was so fed up that it was almost a relief to get going and try to get it over with this time at any rate.

We took off again and, having circled Folkestone, we started out towards Boulogne. The C.O. was flying below with two other machines, in order to do the actual "spotting", while the other nine machines (of which I was one) flew above and behind to guard him and look out for enemy fighters.

In a matter of four or five minutes, I saw Boulogne ahead, and we turned right and flew down the coast to the mouth of the Somme, where we turned inland towards Abbeville, and started to dive at very high speed.

As we approached the aerodrome, a very accurate burst of A.A. fire appeared just in front of us and I swerved to the right and climbed slightly. We soon passed out of range of the battery and the C.O., having inspected Abbeville, turned right for Rouen. From now onwards we could expect enemy fighters, and we scanned the sky anxiously, looking above and behind us almost the whole time. But none appeared, and soon I could see the Seine ahead, winding down to the coast in great S bends.

Only a few weeks before, the bitterest fighting of the war had taken place in the countryside below us, along the banks of the Seine. But it all looked very peaceful that evening, and, travelling at the height and great speed that we were going, I could see no signs of the great struggle that had just finished.

We flew over Rouen aerodrome and then turned north for Dieppe and the coast. We were on the last lap now! The coast loomed up ahead, and a moment later I gave a great sigh of relief as we left French soil behind us. But our troubles were not quite over, for after we were a mile or so from the coast another very accurate burst of A.A. fire came up from a flak ship anchored off Dieppe. This burst came up just ahead of us and rocked several machines violently, though no damage was done.

Shortly after, we crossed the English Coast at Dungeness and turned up towards Folkestone. Gosh, it was good to be back!

We landed and found that the cook had left the mess, so we had to cook ourselves some eggs and bacon. But we just didn't care a hang about anything, and sat and ate our meal and chatted away and felt gloriously happy after the strain of the last 24 hours!

Our stay at Northolt was now almost up because on Thursday morning, July 4th, the enemy bombed Portland.

There was no fighter opposition from us, and so orders came through later in the morning that 609 were to move to Warmwell aerodrome as reinforcements.

We were very pleased about this – not many people like Northolt and whilst there, it was always possible that one would get another of those accursed French patrols! So, we thought that we were well out of it.

The squadron accordingly moved down on the Thursday afternoon, but I stayed behind as it was my day off, and I had to have another medical board about my knee to see that it was now okay. So, I spent the night at Hampstead with D. and turned up at Kingsway the following morning.

I was prodded and pushed and altogether thoroughly "vetted" and pronounced A1, though the doctor was a bit shaken to hear that I had already been flying, as I had not been passed as fit.

So, I went out to Northolt again, and flew down to Warmwell that evening. It seemed grand to be back again, and Michael and

Gordon immediately resumed their mild "affaires" with one or two W.A.A.F.s which had been interrupted when we left in April.

We were the only squadron in that sector at the time, and so did not get any time off, and got up at 3.30 a.m. and went to bed again about 11.30 p.m., altogether a pretty long day.

We had a number of alarms and went out into Weymouth Bay as hard as we could hoping to see some enemy, but I think most of these scares were quite without foundation and after a day or so, I came to the conclusion that I might spend months at this game and never see any action. How little I knew!

On the Sunday we moved up to Middle Wallop (unlovely name) – a new aerodrome between Salisbury and Andover.

This is a very good strategic base for the defence of both Southampton and Portland, and it was to be our home for some time to come.

We continued, however, to use Warmwell as an advanced base and we flew down at dawn every day and returned to Wallop at dusk.

I was sharing a room with Peter Drummond-Hay, and we rose as usual on the Tuesday morning, July 9th, and had an early breakfast – 4.30 a.m. – then flew down to Warmwell in very bad weather.

At about 9.00 a.m. the report came through that a German machine was attacking ships in the bay, so Drummond and I took off to investigate. The clouds were so low that they were actually covering the hills between us and the sea, but we found a gap just where the Weymouth road runs through the little valley. We roared through this gap just above the road (we heard later that two cyclists were so alarmed by these two Spitfires racing through just above their heads that they threw themselves into the ditch!) and then found ourselves in Weymouth Bay.

But it was a false alarm as usual, and so, rather disappointed, we turned back to Warmwell. I think that it was this incident which caused us (and Drummond in particular) to distrust even more the reports that we were getting, which may well have been a contributory cause to the tragedy which occurred later in the day.

It is only fair to say, however, that this was a completely new sector (no attacks here had been visualised till the Germans gained possession of the French Coast) and when a few days later the Operations Room started to function correctly, matters improved enormously.

So, we landed at Warmwell, and sat in the tent again, and listened to the rain outside and Drummond and I fixed to go up to London together on the following day in his car, as we both had the day off and he was going up to see his wife.

At about 4 p.m., Gordon Mitchell took off to inspect the weather, which was now improving slowly. Unfortunately, when coming into land, he misjudged his approach, and hit the propeller of another machine underneath him on the ground. His Spitfire stalled, and sat down very heavily on one wing and broke the undercarriage. Gordon got out quite unhurt, but very fed up.

At about 6.30 p.m. we were ordered to patrol Weymouth, and so Drummond, Michael and I took off. Drummond leading.

We circled Weymouth for about three quarters of an hour, and saw nothing at all. Drummond was getting very fed up with this apparently unnecessary flying, and we circled round Warmwell and asked permission to land. We were told, however, to continue our patrol and turned out again over Weymouth at about 7,000 feet. A moment later, looking out towards the left, I saw an aircraft dive into a layer of cloud about 2 miles away and then reappear. I immediately called up Drummond on the Radio Telephone (R.T.) and told him and he swung us into line astern, and turned left towards the enemy.

We had been told to expect two or three enemy aircraft, but a moment later I saw one or two more appear and recognised them as Junkers 87 dive bombers. I immediately turned on my reflector sights, put my gun button onto "Fire", and settled down to enjoy a little slaughter of a few Ju. 87s, as they are rather helpless machines.

I was flying last on the line, and we were now travelling at very high speed, and rapidly approaching the enemy, when I happened to look round, behind and above, and to my intense surprise and dismay, saw at least nine Messerschmitt 110s about 2,000 feet above us. They were just starting to dive on us when I saw them, and as they were diving, they were overtaking us very rapidly.

This completely altered the situation. We were now hopelessly outnumbered, and in a very dangerous position and altogether I began to see that if we were not jolly quick, we should all be dead in a few seconds.

I immediately called up Drummond and Michael and shouted desperately "Look out behind, Messerschmitts behind", all the time looking over my shoulder at the leading enemy fighter, who was now almost in range.

But though I kept shouting, both Drummond and Michael continued straight on at the bombers ahead, and they were now almost in a range and about to open fire.

I've never felt so desperate or so helpless in my life as when, in spite of my warnings, these two flew steadily on, apparently quite oblivious of the fact that they were going to be struck down from the rear in a few seconds.

At that moment, the leading Messerschmitt opened fire at me, and I saw his shells and tracer bullets going past me. I immediately did a very violent turn to the left and dived through a layer of cloud just below.

I emerged from the cloud going at very high speed – probably over 400 m.p.h. – and saw a Ju. 87 just ahead of me. I opened fire (my first real shot of the war!) and he seemed to fly right through my tracer bullets, but when I turned round to follow him, he had disappeared.

I then climbed up into the cloud again and fired without result at an Me. 110 above me. He turned away immediately and I lost him.

At that moment I saw dimly a machine moving in the cloud on my left and flying parallel to me.

I stalked him through the cloud and when he emerged into a patch of clear sky, I saw that it was a Ju. 87. I was in an ideal position to attack, and opened fire and put the remainder of my ammunition – about 2,000 rounds – into him at very close range.

Pieces flew off the fuselage and cockpit covering, a thin stream of smoke appeared from the engine and a moment later he burst into flames and dived down vertically. Somewhat fascinated by the sight, I followed him down and saw him hit the sea with a great burst of white foam. He disappeared immediately, and apart from the patch of foam there was no sign that anything had happened. The crew made no attempt to get out and there is no doubt that they were killed by my first burst of fire.

I had often wondered what my feelings would be when killing somebody like this, especially when seeing them go down in flames. I was rather surprised to reflect afterwards that my only feeling had been one of considerable elation – and a sort of bewildered surprise because it had all been so easy.

I turned back for the coast – we were about 10 miles out to sea by this time – and started to call up Drummond and Michael on the R.T. But there was no response, and as far as Drummond was concerned, I was already calling to the void.

Moments later I saw another Spitfire flying home on a very erratic course, obviously keeping a very good look behind. I joined up with it and recognised Michael and together we bolted for the English Coast like a couple of startled rabbits.

Everybody was very pleased when we got back and full of congratulations, as it was the first machine the squadron had definitely shot down since Dunkirk.

Michael had left his R.T. in the "Transmit" position instead of "Receive" and so had not heard my warning shouts at the beginning of the action.

Fortunately for him, however, he turned it over just in time and heard me say "Messerschmitt". He whipped round and found himself being attacked by three Me. 110s. He had very great difficulty in escaping, got into a spin, recovered, and then spun the other way! – and came home having fired almost all his rounds at various Me. 110s and Ju. 87s, though without being able to see any results.

He last saw Drummond about a mile away, being attacked by several enemy fighters, but could not go to his aid owing to his own troubles.

As soon as our machines were refuelled and re-armed, six of us flew out into the bay to look for Drummond.

But there was no sign of him at all, and his body was never recovered.

I think there is no doubt that he also had left his R.T. on "Transmit" and so did not hear my warnings, or else perhaps he was thinking that there were only very few enemy, as we had been told, and therefore the possibility of attack from the rear simply did not occur to him. There had been so many false alarms that he was rather in the frame of mind – "nothing can ever happen at Weymouth".

We took off just before dusk to return to Wallop. Gordon could not come as he had damaged his machine earlier in the day and I left him standing outside the tent, looking rather disconsolate because he had not been able to take part in the action with Michael and me. It was the last time I ever saw him.

I went up to my room at Wallop. Everything was just the same as Drummond and I had left it only 18 hours before – his towel was still in the window where he had thrown it during a hurried dressing. But he was dead now. I simply could not get used to such sudden and unexpected death, and there flashed across my mind the arrangements we had made to go up to town together on the following day. It all seemed so ironical, so tragic, so futile.

I felt that I could not see sleep in that room again, and so I took my things and went into Gordon's bed next door and slept there.

But I could not get out of my head the thought of Drummond, with whom we had been talking and laughing that day, now lying in the cockpit of his wrecked Spitfire at the bottom of the English Channel.

I felt much better next morning and caught the afternoon train up to London, where I met D. and we had our usual very pleasant "evening off" together.

I got back to Wallop at lunchtime the following day, Thursday, July 11th, and heard that Pip Barran and Gordon been killed that morning. The whole squadron were down at Warmwell and apparently a lot of fighting was going on all along the South Coast.

I could get no details of what had happened, and I sat alone in the mess all afternoon, feeling more miserable and more stunned than I had ever felt before.

Everybody arrived back after dark, dog tired and utterly depressed. I shall never forget seeing them all come into the mess – people who normally appeared not to have a care in the world, just flopped into chairs and sat there and said not a word.

I rang up D. and told her the news and I think that she was as shocked as I was. She had only met Pip on a few occasions, but of course knew Gordon very well indeed.

What had happened in the morning was this: a ship was being bombed by a fairly large enemy formation south of Portland, and five Spitfires led by Pip took off to go to the spot.

They saw the enemy formation while they were still some distance away – in the usual German formation of bombers below and fighters guarding them above.

Pip detached two machines to try and hold off the enemy fighters (of which there were at least 20) while he led the other two Spitfires (Gordon being one) against the enemy bombers below which were attacking the ship.

It was hopeless from the very start. The fighters had dived down on top of our small formation and everybody was separated immediately. Gordon was not seen again by anybody. After a brief but very sharp fight (during which two enemy dive bombers were almost definitely destroyed) the enemy formation departed, and Blayney saw a Spitfire flying back towards the coast going very slowly and with smoke pouring from it.

This was Pip. A moment later he jumped out, opened his parachute and dropped into the water. Blayney circled round him but it gave no sign of recognition and shortly after, when a boat picked him up, he died as soon as they got him on board.

He had been hit twice in the right leg and was also burnt, but it was probably the shock of being for so long in the water that killed him. I think that if he had dropped on land and been attended to quickly, he would have been quite ok, because he was incredibly strong and tough.

An immediate search for Gordon was made both by aeroplanes and also naval launches etc. from Portland, but he was not found.

It is difficult to describe my feelings during the next few days. We had lost three pilots in 36 hours, all of them in fights in which we had been hopelessly outnumbered, and I felt that there was really nothing left to care about, because obviously from the law of probability one could not expect to survive many more encounters of a similar nature.

When one thinks of the losses sustained in war – particularly by the Army – to lose three people in two days seems very trifling. But in a squadron, there are so few pilots and it really seems more like a rather large family than anything else, and therefore three deaths at once seems very heavy indeed.

Again, compared with the experiences of squadrons during the fighting in France, such losses were small, because some squadrons in France were wiped out almost to a man in a few days.

But they were taking part in heavy and continuous fighting where one expects losses, and also they were destroying much greater numbers of Germans than they themselves were losing, so they could feel, to put it bluntly, that they were getting value for money, which is a very big factor in maintaining spirits and morale.

But our losses had been sustained in two small encounters and we had hardly anything to count against it, in the way of enemy shot down.

So quite apart from the death of one's friends we all felt very depressed and miserable, because obviously things weren't going well.

Gordon's death in particular made a very deep impression on me, because I knew him very much better than I knew Pip, and he, Michael and I had spent the whole war together, and were so accustomed to being together that I could not then (and still cannot now) get used to the idea that we should not see Gordon again, or spend any more of our gay evenings together, or rag him about the moustache of which he was so proud.

He was a very delightful person – possibly rather inclined to be moody at times, but generally a very gay and charming companion, and always exceedingly generous, both as regards material matters and – more important still – in his outlook and views.

He was also a brilliant athlete, a Cambridge Hockey Blue and Scotch International. It always used to delight me to watch Gordon playing any game, whether hockey, tennis or squash because he played with such a natural ease and grace – the unmistakable signs of a first-class athlete.

He was the second Old Leysian to be killed in the air during this war.

But if Gordon's death was a greater shock to me personally, Pip's death was a terrible blow to the squadron.

He was more than a mere member of the squadron – you might almost say that he was the foundation stone upon which it was formed and built.

He was one of the first people to join the squadron when it was started, and he was, I think, easily the outstanding personality of us all. I don't think anybody could mention 609 without immediately thinking of Pip, and his death in the face of such overwhelming odds was characteristic of a very brave and resolute man.

I admired the C.O. very much in these difficult days. He flew as much as everybody else, never batted an eyelid and remained as imperturbable and serene as ever.

It was a very fine example of what can be done by one man's courage and determination, and very shortly matters began to improve, as other fighter squadrons were sent to the South West to reinforce us.

The lesson about going out in such small numbers had also been learnt, and from now onwards we generally flew as a complete squadron, which is a very much more formidable and powerful adversary than three aircraft only.

Two days later, three of us – Beaumont, Blayney, and myself – took off from Wallop in cloudy weather to intercept a lone enemy aircraft which was on a reconnaissance flight.

We flew for some minutes on a given course and were then told by operations room "Look out for him now on your left". A moment later both Jarvis Blayney and I saw him up in the clouds on our left just as "operations" had forecast. Beau, who was leading, did not see him, and so after a few seconds I broke away from formation and went hard after the Dornier with Blayney just behind me.

We opened right up to emergency full throttle, and overhauled the Dornier very rapidly. He didn't see us coming till I was about 400 yards away, and then he turned and ran hard for the nearest cloud with black smoke coming from both engines as an indication that he was also "flat out".

The rear gunner opened fire at me and I could see his tracer flicking past like little red sparks, but he was very inaccurate and a moment later I opened fire and am certain that I killed him immediately, as there was no more return fire and I saw my bursts go right into the fuselage. Blayney said later he was certain that I had shot him down as he also saw my fire going right into the Dornier.

However, the cloud loomed up ahead and a second later the Dornier vanished. I turned left hoping to intercept him on the other side of the cloud, but did not see him again. Blayney had three short bursts at him in gaps in the cloud, but unfortunately lost him also, and so a rather badly damaged Dornier got away safely. Had the cloud been only ½ a mile further away, I think we should have got him easily.

On July 19th, Dorothy came down to Andover for a couple of days and I managed to get most of the time off, so we passed a very pleasant time.

Two days later news came through that Gordon's body had been washed up near Newport on the Isle of Wight.

The station ambulance went down from Wallop and collected the body, and on Thursday, July 25th, exactly a fortnight after his death, I travelled up in the ambulance to Letchworth for his funeral.

His death had been an absolutely overwhelming tragedy for his parents, for he was an only child. I think they felt that after his loss there was really very little left to live for. But they were marvellously brave about it and very kind to me, and touchingly grateful for the letter I had written to them, giving all the known details of Gordon's death, and the approximate time it occurred etc.

The service was very short and simple and he was buried in a lovely little country church near Letchworth. Mr. Bisseker, a very old friend of the Mitchells, came over from Cambridge to conduct the service.

I went up to London after the funeral and spent the night at Hampstead with D. and returned to Wallop the next day.

All through July and early August we used to regularly get the unpopular task of escorting convoys up and down the Channel.

The Germans at that time were concentrating mainly on attacking shipping rather than land objectives, and some very fierce fights used to occur when they bombed the ships.

We loathed this work – the weather was brilliant and the Huns invariably used to attack out of the sun, and sometimes took the escorting fighters completely by surprise.

Also, we were always outnumbered, sometimes by ridiculous odds and a lot of pilots were lost. Many of these were drowned without doubt, when their machine was hit and they descended into the water

10 or 15 miles from land, and were not found despite all the searching that took place afterwards.

Two days after Gordon's funeral on July 27th, a convoy was in Weymouth Bay and a German force approached, and we, along with another Hurricane squadron, went to intercept it. A very confused action followed, in which most of us never saw or engaged the enemy, but we lost one pilot, Buchanan, who was almost certainly shot down by Messerschmitt 109s (hereafter referred to as Me. 109).

We went out to search for him afterwards, and saw something in the water and directed the patrol boat to it as it looked like a parachute, but actually it was a stray barrage balloon in the water. All this occurred very uncomfortably close to the French Coast – we were 40 or 50 miles out from England – and I was exceedingly glad to get back again.

I think Buck's death was also very largely due to inexperience and faulty tactics. We had not yet learnt that it did not pay to go out to sea to meet the enemy but to let them come to us. Also, we did not realise the importance that height meant. Afterwards we used to get as high as possible before going into action. This is the whole secret of success in air fighting.

But Buck's death was another in the series of unnecessary losses against which we had very little to show in the way of success and I think that we all felt very depressed and discouraged.

He was a jolly good chap and a very sound pilot.

However, we learned a lesson from these deaths, though it seems so terrible that in a war, experience is almost always gained at the expense of other men's lives.

But the end of July came, and with it the end of our bad luck, for the time being at any rate. August was to produce many successes, and at least one brilliant victory.

Volume II

August 1940

On July 29th, I got some leave and so Dorothy and I went up to Huddersfield where we spent a very pleasant four days and managed to see quite a lot of people.

On the last day of my leave, we returned to London, where we had a very good dinner, saw Leslie Henson's show, and altogether enjoyed the evening very much indeed.

There were several changes in the squadron when I got back. Four of the original Yeadon pilots had been posted away as instructors as they were all about 30 years of age, and that seems to be too old for fighter pilots.

We had a new Flight Commander in B Flight – MacArthur, who had been a test pilot at Farnborough for two years. Before that he had done a lot of civil flying, including some long-distance flights with Campbell Black, and as a matter of fact "Mac" still holds the London to Baghdad record.

There were also several new pilots including two Poles and three Americans, and altogether the flying personnel of the squadron were now a very much younger and more vigorous and dashing crowd.

I think that these changes played quite a big part in bringing to an end our run of bad luck, because from now onwards we started on an almost unbroken series of successes and victories.

But in less than a year, 609 had completely altered its personnel and character. We had a new C.O. and of the 15 original members of the squadron, only four were now left.

Four others had been posted away to training units and seven had been killed at Dunkirk or Weymouth. Only Michael Appleby, John

Dundas and myself were left, and we were joined a few days later by Geoff Gaunt, who had just finished his course at Cranwell. It was grand to have him back and be together again and Michael and I managed to get Geoff put into B Flight with us, and so for the next six weeks we flew together, and went out on most evenings to the "Mucky Duck" for a little beer and altogether enjoyed life very much in spite of the intense activity that prevailed.

The first week of August 1940 was very quiet indeed and apart from a few enemy machines that flew over at a very great height for reconnaissance and photography, nothing stirred at all. We used to go up after these machines and chased after them over most of South Western England, but they always flew so high and so fast that we were never able to make any interceptions or even to see one. It is not till you go hunting after single machines like this, that you realise the vastness of the sky, and how easy it is, even on a clear day, to miss one aircraft or even a whole squadron in the enormous spaces above.

We had a private and somewhat jocular theory that this unnatural peace was due to Goering having given the whole German Air Force a week's leave, to get them fit for "things to come"!

Certainly, it was the lull before the storm.

The Intelligence reports that we got every day told of the efforts the Germans were making to establish themselves at all the captured aerodromes in Northern France, Holland and Belgium, and obviously preparations were being made on the very greatest scale in order to launch a very heavy air offensive against this country.

I don't know whether many people yet realise fully the great strategical advantages gained by Germany through her occupation of the Low Countries and France.

Hitherto, the Germans had been forced to fly big distances in order to reach this country, whereas we possessed advanced bases in France from which it was only a short flight into the heart of the enemy industrial areas. But we never used these advantages when they were in our grasp and for the first eight months of the war there was no bombing of land targets by either side.

When the big German attack was launched in the West the tables were turned immediately. We lost our advance bases and the enemy gained theirs. Nor was this the end of the misfortunes that fell upon us as a result of the disasters in France. A very big proportion of the German Air Force is composed of Messerschmitt 109s and Junkers 87 dive bombers, both of which are essentially short-range machines and could not possibly operate against England from German bases. But their weight could now be thrown into the struggle, and so instead of meeting Heinkel and Dornier bombers over this country, and being able to inflict wholesale slaughter on them, we had to face very large numbers of escorting Messerschmitts which had to be tackled first. This made the work of our fighter squadrons much more difficult and dangerous, and certainly saved the Germans from the murderous losses which they would have suffered had they sent over unescorted bombers.

Anyway, as it turned out, even their escorting fighters did not manage to save the bombers, and very large numbers were shot down.

And so we enjoyed a few days of peace and did quite a lot of practice flying and attacks, and waited for the storm to break.

At this time, we were still working under an arrangement whereby we lived at Middle Wallop and spent every third day down at Warmwell which was the advanced base. We took it in turns with two other squadrons.

On August 8th, we were down at Warmwell, and soon after dawn we were ordered to patrol a convoy off the Needles. It was a very clear day with a brilliant sun – just the sort of day that the Germans love, because they come over at a very big height and dive down to attack out of the sun.

By doing this, cleverly, they used to render themselves almost invisible until the attack was delivered. We hate these clear days and always pray for some high cloud to cover the sun.

This convoy was a very big one, escorted by several destroyers and balloons towed from barges in order to stop low dive bombing.

I remember thinking at the time that there was obviously going to be a lot of trouble that day, because this convoy was far too large a prize for the Hun to miss. How right I was!

However, nothing happened on our first patrol and after about an hour we returned to Warmwell.

About 11.30 a.m. six of us were ordered off again, but one turned back almost immediately with oxygen trouble, so there were only five of us.

We steered out towards the convoy, which was now about 12 miles south of Bournemouth. There was a small layer of cloud and while dodging in and out of this, Mac and I got separated from the other three, and a moment later we also lost each other.

While looking around to try and find them, I glanced out towards the convoy and saw three of the balloons falling in flames. Obviously an attack was starting and I climbed above the cloud layer and went towards the convoy at full throttle, climbing all the time towards the sun so that I could deliver my attack with the sun behind me.

I was now about five miles from the convoy and could see a big number of enemy fighters circling above, looking exactly like a swarm of flies buzzing round a pot of jam. Below them the dive bombers were diving down on the ships and great fountains of white foam were springing up where their bombs struck the water. I could see that one or two ships had already been hit and were on fire.

I was now at 16,000 feet above the whole battle and turned around to look for a victim. At that moment a Hurricane squadron appeared on the scene, and attacked right into the middle of the enemy fighters, which were split up immediately, and a whole series of individual combats started covering a very big area of the sky.

I saw several machines diving down with smoke and flames pouring from them, and then I perceived a Me. 109 flying about 4,000 feet below me.

I immediately turned and dived down on him – he was a sitting target – but before I got to him a Hurricane appeared and shot him down in flames.

I was very annoyed! I looked round but the attack was finished and the enemy were streaming back towards the French Coast, where it was very unwise to follow them.

Three ships in the convoy were blazing away fiercely and destroyers were taking off the crews. All the balloons had been shot down. I turned back for the English Coast and landed at Warmwell, to find everybody back safely and that the C.O., Michael Appleby and John Curchin had each destroyed an Me. 110, while Mac had shot down two Ju. 87 dive bombers. He would have gotten an Me. 110 also and had got his sights on it but nothing happened when he pressed his trigger. His ammunition was finished! So, a very lucky Me. 110 lived to fight another day.

Mac was very pleased about this fight and certainly a bag of two for one's first action is very good. But it made him rather overconfident and for the next few days he regarded the German Air Force rather as an organization which provided him with a little target practice and general harmless amusement. He soon learnt!

But that evening when we again patrolled the convoy, he led Michael and me almost over to Cherbourg in search of enemy fighters and frightened us considerably. Finally, I called him up on the R.T. and politely pointed out that we were now 50 miles out to sea and that the French Coast was looming up ahead. So, he turned back with great reluctance!

On August 11th, there occurred our first really big action of the war.

We were again down at Warmwell and about 11.30 a.m. we were ordered to patrol over Weymouth Bay. Several other squadrons soon joined us and altogether it looked as though it was going to be a big show.

Shortly afterwards, we saw a big enemy fighter formation out to sea, and went out to attack it, climbing the whole time as they were flying at about 24,000 feet. Some Hurricanes (these Hurricanes were very probably 601 Squadron, including Julian Smithers and John McGrath. Julian was posted Missing after this fight off Portland and no trace of him was ever found) were already attacking the Messerschmitts and the latter had formed their usual defensive circle, going round and round on each other's tails, thus making an attack rather difficult, as if you attack an enemy there is always another enemy behind you. We were now about a thousand feet above the Me.s at about 25,000 feet when the C.O. turned round and the whole of 609 went down to attack.

We came down right on top of the enemy formation, going at terrific speed, and as we approached them, we split up slightly, each pilot selecting his own target.

I saw an Me. 110 ahead of me going across in front. I fired at him but did not allow enough deflection and my bullets passed behind him. I then closed in on him from behind and fired a good burst at practically point-blank range. Some black smoke poured from his port engine and he turned up to the right and stalled. I could not see what happened after this as I narrowly missed hitting his port wing.

There were many more enemy fighters round me and a terrific fight was going on. I couldn't see another target in a good position for me to attack, and it was rather an unhealthy spot in which to linger so I turned and dived back to the coast and landed at Warmwell to refuel and rearm.

Everybody came streaming back in ones and twos, and to my surprise, nobody was missing. It seemed too good to be true that we should all be safe after such a fierce scrap. We had shot down about five Me. 110s and several more (like mine) were probably destroyed, but it is almost impossible (and very unwise) to stay and see definite results in the middle of such a mix up. All that you can do is to fire a good burst at some enemy and then, hit or miss, get away quickly.

Some bombers had got through to Weymouth and Portland and there was a great column of smoke rising from a blazing oil tank, but no very serious damage had been done. The Germans, in spite of the great numerical superiority, had suffered very considerable losses.

Mac came back feeling rather shaken. He had not shot anything down but had been attacked by two Me.s and in his efforts to get away, his Spitfire got into a spin and he came down about 5,000 feet before he could recover.

From now onwards he was a very wise and successful Flight Commander, and never went out looking for unnecessary trouble!

The following day, August 12th, a very heavy attack was made on Portsmouth and the Dockyard.

At midday I was due for 24 hours leave, and I was having a bath and shave in my room at about 11.00 a.m. when somebody rushed up and said that we had been called to Readiness. I hastily wiped the soap off my face and we all got into our cars and went down to dispersal point. A few moments later the order came through to take off and patrol Portsmouth.

I suddenly found that my R.T. was "dead" owing to some slight fault and so had to stay behind while the rest of the squadron took off and headed south.

The adjustments to my R.T. took about five minutes and I then took off by myself and flew off in the direction of Southampton and Portsmouth. I could not see any signs of the rest of the squadron, and as a matter of fact I did not see them during the action.

The Dockyard at Portsmouth had been hit and one or two very big fires were going. I saw some A.A. fire over to the left and flew towards it, when I saw three very large formations of enemy fighters circling off the Isle of Wight. They were in three layers from about 20,000 feet up to 27,000 feet.

I climbed above the middle layer which was composed of Me. 110s and when in position above them, I dived down into the middle of the circle.

As I was going down, I selected a target and blazed away at him for a few seconds, and saw my bullets either hitting him or passing just behind him. I flashed right through the German formation, just missing a collision with one fighter, and continued my dive for another 3,000 feet when I pulled out of the dive to look round.

At that moment an Me. 110, enveloped in a sheet of flame, dropped past within 200 yards of me.

I don't know if this was my victim or not, but I rather think it was as I had seen no other British fighters in action when I attacked.

After pulling out of the dive, I looked round and saw a lot of Huns all round and above me and decided that the sooner I removed myself the better it would be!

So, I turned over on to my back and dived away almost vertically at over 500 m.p.h. towards the English Coast and landed at Wallop. Once again, everybody had got back safely and we had destroyed six or seven Huns definitely and several more probables.

That evening Mac, Noel Agazarian and I went up to town where we met D. and had a very hilarious dinner.

Michael also met us, and we all parted in very good form at about 11.30 p.m. It seemed so funny to be dining peacefully in Piccadilly only a few hours after such a desperate fight!

The following morning, I met Michael in Piccadilly at 8.30 a.m. and we drove back to Wallop together, and at midday the squadron flew down to Warmwell. The date was August 13th, a very lucky 13th for us as it happened.

At about 4.00 p.m. that afternoon we were ordered to patrol Weymouth at 15,000 feet. We took off, thirteen machines in all, with the C.O. leading and climbed up over Weymouth. After a few minutes I began to hear a German voice talking on the R.T. – faintly at first and then growing in volume. By a curious chance this German raid had a wavelength almost identical with our own, and the voice we heard was that of the German commander talking to his formation as they approached us across the Channel. About quarter of an hour later we saw a large German formation approaching below us. There were a number of Junkers 87 dive bombers escorted by Me. 109s above, and also some Me. 110s about two miles behind; about 60 machines in all.

The other Warmwell Squadron, No.152, attacked the Me. 110s as soon as they crossed the coast and they never got through to where we were.

Meanwhile the bombers with their fighter escort still circling above them, passed beneath us. We were up at almost 20,000 feet in the sun and I don't think they ever saw us till very last moment. The C.O. led us round in a big semi-circle so that we were now behind them and we prepared to attack.

Mac, Novi (one of the Poles), and I were flying slightly behind and above the rest of the squadron, guarding their tails, and at this moment I saw about five Me. 109s pass just underneath us.

I immediately broke away from the formation, dived on to the last Me. 109 and gave him a terrific burst of fire at very close range. He burst into flames and spun down for many thousands of feet into the clouds below, leaving behind him a long trail of black smoke.

I followed him down for some way and could not pull out of my dive in time to avoid going below the clouds myself. I found that I was about five miles north of Weymouth and then saw a great column of smoke rising from the ground a short distance away. I knew perfectly well what it was and went over to have a look. My Me. 109 lay in a field – a tangled heap of wreckage burning fiercely but with the black crosses on the wings still visible.

I found out later that the pilot was still in the machine. He had made no attempt to get out while the aircraft was diving and he had obviously been killed by my first burst of fire. He crashed just outside a small village and I could see everybody streaming out of their houses and rushing to the spot.

I climbed up through the clouds again to rejoin the fight and there was nothing to be seen, and so I returned to Warmwell where all the ground crews were in a great state of excitement as they could hear a terrific fight going on above the clouds but saw nothing except several German machines falling in flames.

All the machines were now coming into land and everybody's eyes were fixed on the wings.

Yes – they were all covered with black streaks from the smoke of the guns – everybody had fired!

There was the usual anxious counting – only ten back – where are the others – they should be back by now – I hope to God everybody's okay – good enough, here they come. Thank God, everybody's ok!

We all stood around in small groups talking excitedly and exchanging experiences. It is very amusing to observe the exhilaration and excitement which everybody betrays after a successful action like this!

It soon became obvious that this had been our best effort yet.

Thirteen enemy machines had been destroyed definitely in about four minutes' glorious fighting. Several more were probably destroyed or damaged, and our only damage sustained was a bullet through somebody's wing.

Just after I broke away to attack my Messerschmitt, the whole squadron had dived right into the centre of the German formation and the massacre started. One pilot looked round in the middle of the action and in one small patch of sky, he saw five German dive bombers going down in flames still more or less in formation!

We also heard the German Commander saying desperately time after time "Achtung, Achtung, Spit and Hurri" – meaning presumably "Look out, look out, Spitfires and Hurricanes".

Novi (or Nowierski as his real name is) got two Me. 109s in his first fight and came back more pleased with himself and more excited than I have ever seen anybody before!

The pilot got out of one of the machines which he attacked, and opened his parachute. Novi, seeing this, promptly went at him with the intention of shooting him also, but was attacked by another

Me. 109 which distracted his attention. We were rather relieved about this, as we never regarded the killing of enemy airmen in this way as being very fair. But the Poles always thought otherwise and nothing that we could say would make them alter their opinion. I must say that after the German treatment of the Poles, the latter were quite entitled to take their revenge.

And so ended this very successful day – the thirteenth day of the month, and thirteen of our pilots went into action, and thirteen of the enemy were shot down. I shall never again distrust the number 13!

As one member of the squadron remarked afterwards "he rather missed the 'glorious twelfth' this year, but the glorious thirteenth was the best day's shooting he ever had"!

I think that August 13th marked a very definite turning point in the squadron's history. Hitherto we had not had many successes and had suffered rather heavy losses and this state of affairs always shakes confidence. But now for the first time, the glorious realisation dawned on us that by using clever and careful tactics, we could inflict very heavy losses on the enemy and get away almost scot-free ourselves. Whenever the squadron went into action in the future, I think that the only question in everybody's mind was not "Shall we get many Huns today?" but rather "How many shall we get today?". There was never any doubt about it.

This success also had a very good effect on all the ground crews, who sometimes had to work very long hours without the excitement that the pilots get. But all the airmen are exceedingly interested in the feats and successes of the squadron, and particularly in the machine which they look after.

When you return after an action, the men always crowd round asking for details and if you able to tell them "One Messerschmitt down" there is great rejoicing.

Altogether, from this time onwards, 609 was an exceedingly good squadron and practically second to none in the whole R.A.F.

The next morning, we left Warmwell for the last time, as No.152 Squadron were now stationed there permanently and, in the future, we always operated from Middle Wallop.

Before leaving, we gave instructions to various airmen to go round all the German aircraft which now littered the district as a result of the previous day's fight and get us some souvenirs.

I wanted a propeller blade or instrument from the dashboard of my Me. 109, but unfortunately it was so completely wrecked that they could only recover a compressed air bottle, which I now have at home.

The day was very cloudy, and soon after lunch the air raid warning sounded at Wallop, and we all dashed out of the mess and went down to the dispersal point where our Spitfires were.

There were no orders for us to take off, though three of our machines were already in the air and circling the aerodrome.

So, we sat in our aircraft and waited. A few minutes later we heard the unmistakable "ooma-ooma" of a German bomber above the clouds. I immediately signalled to my ground crew to stand by, as I did not intend to sit on the ground and be bombed! I kept my finger on the engine starter button and waited expectantly.

Almost immediately the enemy bomber – a Junkers 88 – broke out of the cloud to the north of the aerodrome turned slightly to get on his course and dived at very high speed towards the hangars. At about 1,500 feet he let go four bombs – we could see them very distinctly as they plunged down – and a second later there was an earth-shaking "Whoom" and four great clouds of dust rose.

All this happened in a matter of seconds only, but by this time everybody had got their engines started and we all roared helter-skelter across the aerodrome. Why there were no collisions I don't know, but we all got safely into the air and turned round to chase the enemy.

But this was unnecessary. One of our Spitfires had already been in the air and attacked the enemy just as he was climbing up after releasing his bombs. He fired all his ammunition at very close range and the Junkers crashed in flames about ten miles away, all the crew being killed.

I certainly admire that German pilot for his coolness and determination, because he made his attack despite the Spitfires that were closing in on him, and he scored a direct hit on our hangar, killing several men and wrecking the squadron offices, along with two Spitfires which were being overhauled.

Altogether a very cool and daring piece of work, even though he only lived about 30 seconds afterwards to enjoy his triumph.

For the rest of the afternoon we had a very exciting and busy time as various Huns were coming over in the clouds to bomb Wallop. I was able to engage two of them – in both cases I spotted them just as they were breaking from cloud and got a good burst at each before losing them again in the cloud.

There were both certainly damaged but nothing more. The main thing was that it stopped them bombing the aerodrome, but during the afternoon one other German managed to hit the hangars and get back into cloud again before any of us could intercept him.

We destroyed two definitely, but unfortunately when everybody landed later that evening Goodwin was missing and he never turned up. We could not understand this as all the fights had taken place near Wallop and they had been so scrappy and disjointed that it seemed almost impossible for anybody (except Huns!) to be killed.

However, the mystery was solved about ten days later when his body was washed ashore on the Isle of Wight. Obviously, he had chased some bomber out to sea and been shot down.

It was a great pity as he was a pleasant chap and his younger brother – also in the R.A.F. – had been killed only six weeks before.

Incidentally, in one of the shot down Heinkels, three very high officers of the German Air Force were found dead. They had probably come over to see how the operations against England were progressing.

I have no doubt that they were suitably impressed!

The following day, August 15th, we had another raid on Wallop in the late afternoon, this time by a fairly big formation of Ju. 88s and Me. 110s.

Through some delay on the part of the Operations Room, we got off the ground only a few minutes before they arrived at the aerodrome, and were unable to intercept them or even to see them until they were practically over the aerodrome, as they dived out of the sun, dropped their bombs and then streamed back towards the coast as hard as they could go. But we were attacking them the whole time and shot down at least five. Oddly enough, less damage was done to the aerodrome by this large raid than on the previous day when only single machines came over.

Most of these German bomber formations rely on one very good bomb aimer in the leading machine. When he gets his sights on, the whole formation releases their bombs and if the aim is accurate, the effect is generally rather devastating. But on this occasion the bomb aimer misjudged by about two seconds and the whole salvo of bombs fell just beyond the aerodrome.

This occasion was the now famous one when I shot down one of our own machines – a Blenheim!

There was a Blenheim fighter squadron stationed at Wallop, they are not fast enough for day fighting but are used a lot for night work as they are fairly large and can carry some of the bulky equipment which is now used for night fighting. Incidentally, they are twin engined machines and very similar in appearance to the Junkers 88.

One of these Blenheims happened to the doing some practice flying near the aerodrome when the attack started and in a fit of rather misguided valour, he fastened himself on to the German formation as it ran for the coast, and started attacking the rear machines.

I was rapidly overhauling the Germans and, when in range, opened fire at the last machine on the line, which happened to be the Blenheim. I hit both engines and the fuselage, one engine stopped immediately, and he made a crash landing at Wallop. Fortunately, the pilot had been saved by the armour plating behind him, and the rear gunner had a bullet through his bottom which doubtless caused him considerable discomfort and inconvenience, but was not serious.

Nothing was said about this mistake as it was certainly not my fault, and equally the Blenheim pilot could scarcely be blamed for his desire to engage the enemy, even though it was rather unwise since his machine was so similar to the Germans.

The Blenheims had sometimes got in our way before, and we had often remarked jokingly "If one of those blasted Blenheims gets in our way again, we'll jolly well put a bullet through his bottom". And now it had come to pass and everybody was very amused (except possibly the rear gunner).

The whole story became very well-known and I was ragged about it for a long time afterwards.

Our other Polish pilot, Osti (his real name being something like Ostaszewski) distinguished himself in this action. He chased an Me. 110, which in its efforts to shake him off dived to ground level and dodged all over the countryside at over 300 m.p.h., even turning round a church steeple. But Osti stuck to him and refused to be shaken off and finally the German, as a last and desperate resort, flew right through Southampton's balloon barrage.

Osti went through after him, caught him up over the Solent and shot him down on the Isle of Wight.

These two Poles, Novi and Osti, were grand chaps and we were all very fond of them.

They had fought in Poland during the desperate months of September 1939 when, in spite of inferior equipment and being hopelessly and tragically outnumbered, they nevertheless resisted to the bitter end, and then escaped through Rumania to France, where they joined l'Armée de l'Air, and again fought till the French collapse, though they were very shabbily treated by the French, who gave them only very obsolete machines to fly.

They told us some astonishing stories (which I believe implicitly) about conditions in France during the disasters in May and June.

They were stationed near Tours, and on the aerodrome were a number of very good new American Curtiss fighters. The Poles, who had been given Moranes which were old and hardly fit to fly, let alone fight, begged to be allowed to fly the Curtiss.

But the French refused, saying they wanted the Curtiss's themselves.

Every day the Germans used to fly serenely over Tours, bomb the city at leisure and fly back again, while nobody raised a finger to stop them, and the French pilots sat in the bar and drank their Vermouth, with a lot of brand-new fighters standing on the aerodrome outside. Incredible but true!

Anyway, Novi and Osti, and several thousand more of their indomitable countrymen, escaped once more from a ravaged country and came over to England. It is easy to imagine their pleasure at finding themselves in a really good squadron, efficiently run with first class equipment. They could now fly the finest fighters in the world and meet their persecutors on equal terms.

They certainly make the most of their opportunities and their delight when they shot down a "bloddy German" was marvellous to see.

They were both very quiet, possessed beautiful manners, were very good pilots and intensely keen to learn our ways and methods. Their hatred of the Germans was quieter and more deadly than I have ever seen before.

They had undergone so much suffering and hardship, and had lost almost everything in life that mattered to them – homes, families, money – that I think the only thing that concerned them now was to get their revenge and kill as many Germans as possible.

They were certainly two of the bravest men I ever knew, and yet they were not exceptional in this respect when compared with other Poles in the R.A.F.

All the squadrons that had Polish pilots posted to them formed an equally high opinion of them, and the feats of the all-Polish Squadron, No. 303, who in five days' fighting over London, destroyed at least 44 German machines as well as probably destroying and damaging many more, must rank as one of the finest achievements in the whole history of the R.A.F.

Such indomitable courage and determination cannot go unrewarded, and when this war is won, we must see that Poland is again restored to her former liberty and freedom, which her sons fought so valiantly to maintain.

After this raid on Wallop, life became much quieter for a short period, and while we had a number of alarms and went up on patrol quite a lot, we did not come into contact with the enemy for some time to come.

In the middle of our "busy time", when every day seemed to bring a bigger and heavier raid to deal with, we used to long for bad weather to come and give us some relief. Now when matters became quieter and we had no fighting, we all got very bored after a few days and longed to shoot down some more Huns. Human nature is never satisfied for long!

At this time, I was still managing to get up to London once or twice a week to meet D.

We used to have some very pleasant dinners, sometimes with Michael and Geoff when they were up in town also.

Serious bombing had not yet commenced in London, and life was still proceeding very much as usual, so after a very good dinner we used to go to a flick or a show and then back to Hampstead for the night. I always had to leave in fairly good time in the morning, in order to catch the 9.30 a.m. train from Waterloo to Andover.

On August 23rd, I managed to get my 24 hours leave as usual and met D. to celebrate the first anniversary of our wedding. We had a very good dinner at Hatchetts, listened to an excellent band, and altogether enjoyed our little celebration very much.

What an eventful year it had been! But in spite of all the worries and anxieties of the present, I think we both felt much happier and more confident than we had done a year previously, when we were married under the shadow of impending war and the whole future seemed so black and full of doubt.

It was still equally uncertain now, but we were getting more accustomed to not thinking in terms of the future, and we had made the necessary mental adjustments to be able to face the worries and doubts.

In this year there have been so much personal happiness, and such good times, so many outstanding people met, and so many new friends made.

There had been the finest flying I have ever had, and the most exciting and wildly exhilarating moments of my life, such as the fight over Weymouth, and that first engagement with the enemy when I dived on to the Junkers 87, and sent it crashing down in flames into the sea.

And on the other hand, there had been so much monotony and anxiety – both inevitable in war – and in the latter part of the year there occurred the tragic deaths of so many gallant friends, among them being some of the finest people I ever knew.

But, on the whole, it had been easily the happiest and certainly the most vivid year of my life. I certainly could not feel now (as I used to feel occasionally before the war) that I should lead an uneventful life and grow into an old man without possessing any really exciting and stirring memories to gladden my old age.

The following day, August 24th, I returned to Wallop. The weather was brilliantly clear again to our intense disgust, and we anticipated a lot of trouble.

Mac was very amusing on the subject of the weather, and always used to scan the sky anxiously looking for clouds. When we saw any rolling up, he used to express great satisfaction and announce that it might keep the "Grim Reaper" at bay for another few days. Mac and his "Grim Reaper" became a stock joke, and if anybody had a narrow escape, we always had to congratulate them on keeping the "Grim Reaper" at bay.

Certainly, it was typical of our contrary and fickle English weather that in a normal summer it is quite impossible to get fine weather for one's holidays, and yet in wartime, when every fine day simply plays into the hands of the German bombers, we had week after week of cloudless blue skies.

Anyway, August 24th proved to be no exception to the general rule, and about 4.00 p.m. we took off with orders to patrol Portsmouth at 10,000 feet. A number of other squadrons were also operating, each at different heights and on this occasion, we were the luckless ones sent low down to deal with any possible dive bombers.

We hated this – it's a much more comforting and reassuring feeling to be on top of everything than right underneath!

Superior height is the whole secret of success in air fighting.

Anyway, "orders is orders" and so we patrolled Portsmouth. Very soon a terrific A.A. barrage sprang up ahead of us, looking exactly like a big number of dirty cotton wool puffs in the sky. It was a most impressive barrage – besides all the guns at Portsmouth, all the warships in the harbour and the Dockyard were firing hard.

A moment later, through the barrage and well above us, we saw a large German formation wheeling above Portsmouth.

We were too low to be able to do anything about it, but they were being engaged by the higher squadrons.

They were now releasing their bombs, and I cannot imagine a more flagrant case of indiscriminate bombing. The whole salvo fell right into the middle of Portsmouth, and I could see great spurts of flame and smoke springing up all over the place. A lot of people were killed in this raid.

We spent a very unpleasant and frightening few minutes right underneath the German formation, praying hard that their fighters would not come down on us.

However, the danger passed, and a very disgruntled squadron returned to Wallop, having seen so many Huns and yet not having fired a single round.

Also, one of our Americans, Andy Mamedoff, was attacked by a Messerschmitt, which in his inexperience he never saw following him, and the Me put a lot of bullets into Andy's machine including one which went right through the armour plating behind his seat. Fortunately, it had just expended its force and apart from giving Andy a good thump in the back it did no further damage. But his machine was badly hit, and he was very lucky to get away with it.

These three Americans – Andy, "Red" Tobin, and "Shorty" Keough, had joined the French Air Force and came over to England in June. They had all been civil pilots in America and had done a lot of flying. But civil flying is one thing and military flying (especially in war) is quite another, and they were very raw and inexperienced when they came to us. However, they were very keen and anxious to learn and soon improved, though they seemed to damage quite a number of Spitfires in doing so!

They were typical Americans – very amusing and altogether excellent company. Our three Yanks became quite an outstanding feature of the squadron. [See Appendix II]

One day the Duke of Kent came down to see us. The Americans were very intrigued about this when they heard of the forthcoming visit – being good Republicans they are always amazingly impressed by royalty! Shorty said, "Say what do we call this guy – dook?" We hastily assured him that "Sir" would be sufficient!

Anyway, the "dook" arrived, shook hands with us all and spoke to us, and had a particularly long chat with Shorty, who, amongst other jobs in a very varied career, had been a professional parachute jumper. Shorty was immensely gratified!

Unfortunately, after about six weeks with us, and just as they were becoming quite good, they were posted away to form an all-American squadron – the Eagle Squadron. We were all very sorry indeed to lose them.

About this time, we received a visit from Lord Trenchard. He is of course more or less the father of the R.A.F. because he commanded it for the last two years of the Great War and then for many years of peace. He chatted to us for quite a long time in a very paternal and charming manner, congratulated us on our successes, and said that the only way to win this war was to give the Hun such hell as he had never had before and would never want again. Altogether a very delightful and distinguished old boy who, in spite of his age, still possessed a very strong gleam in his eye. We were all duly impressed!

On August 25th, we took off in the afternoon and patrolled Swanage, as a large German raid was approaching the coast.

It might be useful here to explain roughly the system of fighter interceptions as conducted by Fighter Command.

All along the coasts of this country there are a number of detector or listening posts which contain some very ingenious and secret equipment. Any aeroplane approaching our coasts is immediately "picked up" by these stations, which are also able to give, fairly accurately, the size of the formation which is on the way i.e. whether it contains 10 or 100 machines.

All this information is passed immediately to the Operations Rooms, who control our fighter squadrons. They now know roughly the number of enemy aircraft involved and can judge fairly accurately the targets they are making for, and they send up our squadrons to patrol that part of the coast which the enemy will cross.

They are of course in constant touch with the squadrons by R.T., and can easily divert them to some other threatened point.

The whole system, which actually is far more complicated and secret than would appear from this rough sketch, is exceedingly effective and thus when the enemy bombers cross these coasts our fighter squadrons are already at a great height and ready to pounce on them.

Anyway, on this particular day we were at 20,000 feet over Swanage and were told that a very big number of enemy aircraft were approaching.

Shortly afterwards we sighted the enemy coming over the coast below us and the C.O. swung us into line astern and manoeuvred into a good position for the attack. Then – down we went. I happened to be almost last on the line and I shall never forget that sight – the long line of Spitfires ahead sweeping down and curling round at terrific speed to strike right into the middle of the German formation. It was superb!

The great weight and fierceness of this onslaught split up the Huns immediately and they scattered all over the place, with our people chasing them right and left. I saw an Me. 110 below me and ahead and dived on to him, going very fast indeed. Unfortunately, I was going too fast and in the heat of the moment I forgot to throttle back, with the result that I came up behind him, had one blind burst at him as he flashed by, and then had to turn away very violently or I should have collided with him. His rear gunner took advantage of my mistake and fired a short burst at me and put a bullet through my wing – the first time that my Spitfire had been hit.

When I turned round and looked for him, he had disappeared and though there was a lot of fighting in progress and machines were turning, diving, and zooming madly all over the sky, I was not in a good position to attack, and a moment later most of the Germans turned back out to sea.

I went as hard as I could for Weymouth thinking that I might pick up something there. As I passed over Warmwell I could see that it had been bombed and a big fire was raging. I got to Weymouth, but the fighting had almost finished there too, though one Me. 109 dived vertically into the sea just off the Chesil Bank and another one, with its engine stopped and a Spitfire watching it carefully, glided down and made a forced landing in a field near the coast. I saw the pilot get out, apparently unhurt, set fire to his machine, and then walk away calmly across the field.

When I got back to Wallop, I found that everybody had got back safely, and we had destroyed six or seven Huns. Various other squadrons and got some victims also and in all 30 Huns were definitely destroyed on this raid. Bombs had been dropped only at Warmwell, where nobody was hurt, some hangars slightly damaged, station sick quarters burnt out, and a few craters made in the aerodrome which were immediately filled in.

Not a very good return for the loss of 30 machines and crews!

This was Geoff's first action and he shot down an Me. 110, together with Noel Agazarian. Officially they were credited with half each!

Osti had an amazing escape in this fight. An Me. 110 got onto his tail and put one cannon shell into his engine where it blew out most of the induction system, while another shell hit the armour plating behind his head, and the explosion almost stunned him.

He managed to get back to Wallop however, with a big hole in his wing as well, but had to land very fast as his flaps were damaged, and he ran through the hedge.

His machine was a complete "write off" but he was quite ok, apart from a headache!

Nothing else of interest occurred in the last few days of August and at the end of the month we were able to add up our score.

This was 56 enemy aircraft definitely destroyed, as well as the number of others probably destroyed or damaged and our only loss was one pilot killed.

Not a bad record for one month!

This result is astonishing when compared with that of the previous month, July, when in a very few engagements only, we lost four pilots and shot down about five Huns – almost equal numbers.

We had now learnt our lessons, though the price of this experience had been the deaths of several of our friends.

We realise now the vital importance of getting above the enemy before going into action; we knew that cool thinking and the element of surprise can more than compensate for inferior numbers, and can sometimes produce astonishing results; we knew from experience that if you attack out of the sun, the enemy will hardly ever see you till the last moment, and vice versa, how essential it is to maintain the most intense vigilance always in order to prevent being surprised oneself.

We also realised the importance of constantly dodging and twisting during a fight because if you steer a straight and steady course for more than about five seconds, a Messerschmitt will probably be sitting just behind you and firing as hard as he can!

But after all this, a very great deal of credit for our changed fortunes was due to the C.O. He came to command the squadron at the beginning of July when, owing to lack of experience, we were not a particularly efficient fighting unit. He was with us all through the bad times, when we lost more than we shot down, and when the morale of the squadron might have gone rapidly from bad to worse. But he flew as much as anybody else, led us skilfully and throughout remained so imperturbable; so confident and so cheerful that he held everybody together by his example.

And so, the end of August found us with a very satisfactory and solid background of success and victory, and we now faced the future with an ample confidence that whatever the Germans might do, we could do it far better.

September 1940

Seotember opened quietly as far as we were concerned, and though we did a number of patrols nothing very much happened. The days were now getting noticeably shorter and we benefited accordingly as we could now be released at dusk – between 7.00 p.m. and 8.00 p.m. – and get out more in the evenings.

A great contrast with the state of affairs at Warmwell in July when, for several days on end, we were on duty (and doing a lot of flying) from 3.30 a.m. till 10.45 p.m.

We were able to do quite a lot of practice flying and I had a lot of dogfights (i.e. single combats) with Geoff.

There was a tremendous rivalry between us and altogether they proved to be most energetic affairs – turning, diving and climbing all over the sky at anything between 300 m.p.h. and 400 m.p.h., in a desperate attempt to get on each other's tails! But dogfighting in a Spitfire is a very tiring business owing to the very high speeds and heavy strains involved, and after about ten minutes we had generally had enough!

So, we flew back to Wallop with honours generally about even.

At the beginning of the month, the London night bombing started to get rapidly worse, and so, rather reluctantly, we decided that D. would have to go north to Huddersfield. This was the only thing to do, but it meant the end of our pleasant evenings every week in town.

From now onwards, we could see each other only on the comparatively rare occasions that I could get up home.

However, on September 7th, John Dundas (who lives at Cawthorne) and I got the Magister and flew up to Yeadon for 24 hours leave. It seemed very odd to be piloting a little aeroplane at 100 m.p.h. again. I really did find it more difficult to fly than a Spitfire, so accustomed had I become to the latter.

Anyway, we did a very neat bit of navigation between us (fighter pilots are not generally renowned for their navigational skill!) and dived over the Dundas household at Cawthorne, and flew over Glenwood where I could see the family waving hard from the lawn.

It was grand to be home again, and I spent a very happy 24 hours and we flew back the following morning. The only incident on the return trip being that Dundas started adjusting his scarf round his neck and it flew away, to his considerable chagrin!

We found everybody in very cheery form when we got back. The first big daylight raid on London had taken place the previous day and 609 had their first fight for about a fortnight, during which time we had become very bored with inactivity. We got about six Huns confirmed, and everybody got back safely (except "Aggy" who had a bullet in his engine and force landed). The whole squadron then adjourned to Gordon Harker's cocktail party in aid of the Spitfire Fund.

They all thought this most appropriate! So altogether we had missed quite a lot of fun!

In the next week or two we flew up to London almost every day – sometimes twice a day – in order to give the overworked London squadrons a helping hand. They certainly needed it – the weight and intensity of these raids exceeded anything ever seen before.

Day after day, great masses of German bombers with enormous fighter escorts tried to battle their way through to the capital.

Sometimes they were beaten back, sometimes a number of the bombers got through, but they always suffered terrible losses.

Day after day, battles of incredible ferocity were taking place, often at a height of five or six miles, and the great conflict raged from Dover, all up through Kent and the Thames Estuary, over the London suburbs and then south again through Sussex to the coast.

Many hundreds of German bombers and fighters littered the fields and countryside of South Eastern England, and yet each morning brought a fresh wave of the enemy aircraft, manned by crews who generally showed a fine determination and doggedness in the face of such murderous losses.

The strain on everybody in Fighter Command was very heavy indeed during this period. Many aerodromes were bombed till hardly a building of any importance was left standing, and yet they continued to function at full operational efficiency. Some squadrons lost almost all their pilots in a matter of a few days and had to be withdrawn in order to be rested and reformed. To many pilots in the London squadrons, the strain at times must have seemed almost unbearable, and yet everybody held out, badly outnumbered though they were, and at the end of a few weeks it was the Luftwaffe and not the R.A.F. who had to cry Halt.

"Hard pounding, gentleman" said the Duke of Wellington at Waterloo, "let us see who pounds the longest".

In this prolonged and bitter encounter, it was certainly the R.A.F. who pounded the longest – and the hardest.

However, we did not get our full share of these battles and though we always went towards London and generally patrolled Guildford or Brooklands, we were often sent off with orders to patrol at a low altitude – about 10,000 feet – in order to deal with any dive bombing or low-level attacks.

This was quite sensible as we had a long way to go from Andover and might not have had sufficient time to get up to very big altitudes before the Germans arrived. The London squadrons, on the other hand, had ample time in which to get up to 25,000 feet or more and therefore got a lot more fighting than we did, as the enemy bombers used to take full advantage of the cloudless skies and do their bombing from about 18,000 feet, while their escorting fighters circled round them and above them at anything up to 30,000 feet.

It was always a rather tricky and unpleasant business attacking the bombers while their fighter escort was still in position above.

Often it was almost impossible to see them because of the blinding sun, but you always knew that they were there – and as soon as they saw a favourable opportunity, they would dive down and attack. Generally, therefore, we had to try and get in one very quick attack on the bombers and then get away or, at any rate, turn round before the fighters arrived on the scene.

Some squadrons used to do head-on attacks at the bombers, approaching them from the opposite direction, firing hard in the split seconds as they drew nearer (their aggregate rate of closing being about 550 m.p.h.) and then pull up quickly at the last moment in order to avoid collision. These tactics, carried out with the utmost recklessness and abandon, were generally very successful in destroying some bombers and, more important still, splitting up the formation so that the machines, separated, could be hunted and shot down far more easily. Moreover, they rather shook the morale of a number of enemy pilots, and many prisoners, when questioned after capture, said how disconcerting and terrifying they found these attacks.

Certainly, after the offensive had been in progress for a few weeks, enemy bombers showed a much greater tendency to jettison their bombs and turn back when attacked, and this was a great contrast to the earlier showing, when attacks were usually pressed home with the utmost determination.

We were patrolling over south-western London one afternoon in early September, during a big raid, and were watching the sky intently, waiting for the Hun to appear. Suddenly somebody said: "Enemy formation above us on the right."

I looked up and a moment later saw the biggest German bomber formation that I had ever seen. Like a great wedge in the sky it moved steadily on, black, menacing, apparently irresistible. Above it, a terrific fight was going on between the German fighters and our own squadrons, but nobody apparently had been able to get near the

1. DMC (centre) and chums on a pre-war skiing holiday in Switzerland. (*All photographs Dilip Sarkar Archive*)

2. DMC, second left, and pals, pre-war skiing trip.

3. Pilot Officer David Moore Crook, Auxiliary Air Force, 1939.

4. Dorothy Middleton, whom DMC married at Lindley Parish Church, Yorkshire, on 23 August 1939. The couple would have three children: Nicholas, Rosemary and Elizabeth.

5. 'Warmwell, April 1940. Back row: Michael Appleby, Sgt Froud, "Greg". Front row: Basil Fisher, John McGrath, Self, Gordon Mitchell, F/Lt Berryman, Roger Forshaw, Bell, Jon Hay, Claude Goldsmith.'

6. A portrait of DMC.

7. Another photograph of DMC.

8. DMC at the controls of his Spitfire. The original, hand-written caption states: 'Me and my beloved Spitfire!'

9. Crook's Spitfire, PR-L, at Northolt. DMC's original caption states: 'July 1st at Northolt. Me and my Spitfire, the evening before our patrol over France.'

10. The same spot at RAF Northolt in May 2021.

11. 'Taken at Northolt, July 1st 1940: John Curchin, Michael Appleby, Pip Barran and Gordon Mitchell.'

12. Pilots of 609 Squadron in August 1940. In the front row, on the left, is DMC, whilst to the right of him is Vernon Charles 'Shorty' Keough.

13. DMC's original caption for this image states: 'Re-arming my Spitfire after the fight on July 9th. A new oxygen bottle is being put in the cockpit.'

14. '13 August 1940. Some of the Squadron just after Weymouth fight. Standing: Red, Osti, G., E., Michael, Frank, the CO, Mac, Sergeant F., Novi and Teeny. In front: Mike, DMC & Mick.'

15. A picture of 609 Squadron's duty board at Warmwell, 13 August 1940.

16. DMC's Spitfire pictured being tended by groundcrew in August 1940. His handwritten caption notes the following: 'Re-arming my Spitfire after the fight above Portland, August 13, 1940.'

17. 'Readiness, September 1940: Shorty, Geoff and DMC'. From front to back are Pilot Officer Vernon Charles 'Shorty' Keough (an American), Pilot Officer Geoffrey Gaunt and Pilot Officer David Moore Crook. One source states that Crook is seen here 'writing his wartime diary'.

18. As DMC himself stated, this image shows him 'Taking off for one of the London battles, September 1940.'

19. The wreckage of the Dornier Do.17Z, F1+FH from 1/KG76, that crashed near Victoria Station on Sunday, 15 September 1940. It had taken off from its base at Nivelles, just south of Beauvais, at 10.05 hours with 27-year-old Oberleutnant Robert Zehbe at the controls. (Historic Military Press)

20. Firemen and ARP personnel deal with the wreckage of Dornier Do.17 F1+FH in front of Victoria Station on 15 September 1940. This is an example of a 'Wirephoto', which was cabled from London to New York for immediate publication. (Historic Military Press)

21. DMC, on the left, with his great friend Pilot Officer Geoffrey Gaunt – shot down over London in flames and killed on 15 September 1940.

22. Geoffrey Gaunt's grave at Salendine Nook Baptist Chapel, Huddersfield, Yorkshire. (Glenn Gelder)

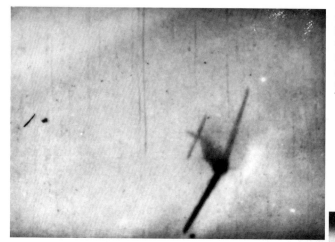

23. A still taken from the camera gun footage of DMC's Spitfire on 30 September 1940. In his memoir he wrote: 'The Me. 109 on fire and turning on his back just before diving into the sea.'

24. Another still taken from the camera gun footage of DMC's Spitfire on 30 September 1940. His original caption states: 'One Me.109 on Sep. 30th on fire and turning on his back just before diving into the sea.'

25. 'The drone.'

26. Pilot Officer Tadek 'Novi' Nowierski.

28. Flying Officer Henry McDonald 'Mac' Goodwin, killed in action 14 August 1940. His brother, Barrie, was killed two months earlier flying Hurricanes with 605 Squadron; the brothers lie buried side-by-side at St Cassian's Chaddesley Corbett, Worcestershire.

27. 'The grey dawn at Wallop (about 0530 am). The CO, Mac, Noel Agazarian, Osdti and Novi.'

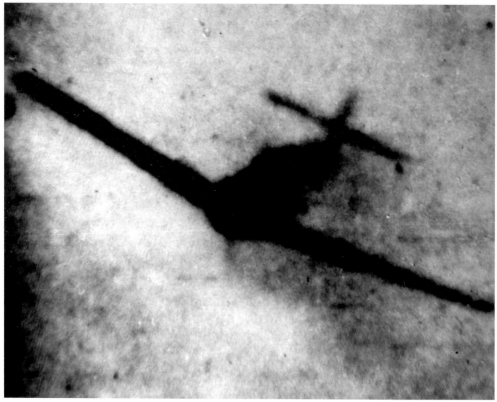

29. An Me. 109 under fire from DMC.

ROYAL AIR FORCE
The King has approved the following awards in recognition of gallantry displayed in flying operations against the enemy:—
DISTINGUISHED FLYING CROSS
Pilot Officer D. M. CROOK, A.A.F.

This officer has led his section with coolness and judgment, and has destroyed six enemy aircraft besides damaging several more.

30. A newspaper cutting that DMC himself kept following the announcement of his award of the Distinguished Flying Cross.

31. DMC, on the right, at Buckingham Palace on 29 February 1941, with (from left) Pilot Officer John Curchin and Flight Lieutenant Frank Howell at their DFC investiture.

32. A formal portrait of DMC having received the DFC.

33. DMC and Spitfire PR-P.

34. Flight Lieutenant Frank Howell DFC and Pilot Officer Sydney Hill celebrate 609 Squadron's 100th kill. The aircraft shot down was a Junkers Ju 88 on 21 October 1940. The original caption states: 'Frank and Sidney [sic] with the swastika from our hundredth Hun.'

35. A portrait of DMC.

36. Another portrait of DMC. Note the Auxiliary Air Force 'A' badges on the collar of his tunic.

37. DMC's portrait by the war artist Cuthbert Orde.

38. Pilot Officer Michael Appleby, also drawn by Orde.

39. A portrait of Flying Officer John Dundas DFC that was also undertaken by Orde. Dundas was shot down and killed over the Isle of Wight on 28 November 1940, having himself shot down, seconds earlier, the German ace Major Helmut Wick.

40. DMC pictured whilst instructing on Hurricanes.

41. Another photograph of DMC taken during his time as an instructor on Hurricanes.

42. DMC the flying instructor and veteran fighter ace.

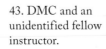

43. DMC and an unidentified fellow instructor.

44. Flight Lieutenant David Moore Crook DFC remains missing and is commemorated on the Runnymede Memorial.

1944
ROYAL AIR FORCE
FLIGHT LIEUTENANT
COOPER H.T.D
COOPER T.N.
COWLEY N.A.T.F
CRABB J.M.
CRAMER O.R.
CROOK D.M. D.F.C
CURTIS R.
DAWSON E.S. D.F.C
DOBSON L.S.
DODSWORTH R.H.
DOYLE K.P.C. D.F.C
DRAYERS P.G.
DRURY H.
DUNFEE G.E.
DUNN R.F
DURINGER A.H. D.F.C. D.F.M
ECCLES G.B. A.F.C
ELLIOTT K.G.
ELLIS J.L.
ELVIN R.G. D.F.C
EMERY J.J.
FEELEY A. D.F.C
FILLEUL P.R.S
FINN J.A.
FITZGERALD C.K. D.F.C
FORD D.R.O. D.F.C
FORD F.J.
FORGAN R.T.
FOX J.D.
FRANCIS E. D.F.C

45. The panel at Runnymede on which Crook is commemorated by name.

your thumb waits expectantly on the trigger, and your eyes watch the gun sights through which in a few seconds an enemy will be flying in a veritable hail of fire.

And all round you, in front and behind, there are your friends too, all eager and excited, all thundering down together into the attack! The memory of such moments is burnt into my mind for ever.

I was flying just behind Miller and he turned slightly left to attack an Me.110 which was coming towards him. But the German was as determined as Miller, and refused to give way or alter course to avoid this head-on attack. Their aggregate speed of closing was at least 600 mph and an instant later they collided.

There was a terrific explosion and a sheet of flame seemed to hang in the air like a great ball of fire. Many little shattered fragments fluttered down and that was all. Miller was killed instantly and

---

We used to have some very pleasant dinners, sometimes with Michael and Geoff when they were up in Town also.

Serious bombing had not yet commenced in London, and life was still proceeding very much as usual, so after a very good dinner we used to go to a flic or a show and then back to Hampstead for the night. I always had to leave in fairly good time in the morning, in order to catch the 9.30 am train from Waterloo to Andover.

On August 23rd I managed to get my 24 hours leave as usual and met J to celebrate the first anniversary of our wedding. We had a very good dinner at Hatchetts, listened to an excellent band, and altogether enjoyed our little celebration very much.

What an eventful year it had been! But in spite of all the worries and anxieties of the present, I think we both felt much happier and more confident than we had done a year previously, when we were married under the shadow

---

place from Weymouth, where they crossed the coast, all up through Somerset to Bristol and then back again. A number of our squadrons were engaged and the Germans suffered fairly heavy losses, though I think on the whole they could claim it was a fairly satisfactory raid.

Shortly after my return, a raid came into Southampton and we took off to intercept it. This was not a very satisfactory action for us — just before we attacked the bombers a lot of Me.109s dived on us from out of the sun and we were split up.

We suffered no casualties and the German pilots can't have been very good — had the positions been reversed and we had dived on them in similar circumstances a lot of them would never have seen the Fatherland again.

In the rather confused action which ensued some of us did not find a target (I was one) and had to return without firing a round.

However some people including

46. Three sample pages of DMC's original hand-written manuscript for *Spitfire Pilot* – and which are published here in this edition.

47. The front cover of the first edition of *Spitfire Pilot* which was published by Faber and Faber in 1942.

48. The late Dorothy Hessling, DMC's widow, photographed at home in Acocks Green, Birmingham, by Dilip Sarkar in 1990.

49. During the Battle of Britain, 609 Squadron was one of two Spitfire squadrons based at Warmwell in Dorset, inland of Weymouth. Several of the Few lie at rest there at Holy Trinity.

50. Amongst the casualties at Holy Trinity is 609 Squadron's Sergeant Alan Feary, killed in action on 7 October 1940 – one of seven pilots lost by 609 Squadron during the Battle of Britain. In DMC's book, the twenty-eight-year old reservist from Derbyshire is referred to simply as 'Sergeant F'.

51. Pilot Officer Rogers Miller – whose fatal collision in combat with a Me. 110 DMC witnessed on 27 September 1940. Miller's story is told in Dilip Sarkar's *Battle of Britain 1940: The Finest Hour's Human Cost* (Pen & Sword, 2020).

52. The crash site near Lymington, Hampshire, of the Me 109E-1 destroyed by Pilot Officer 'Novi' Nowierski on 15 October 1940, an incident witnessed by DMC and referred to in his manuscript. The German pilot, Obergefrieter A Pollach of 4/JG2 baled out and was captured.

53. In 2015, Dilip Sarkar and friends excavated Pollach's crash-site, discovering innumerable small fragments, such as these pieces of engine casing and perspex, indicating that Pollach's cannon-less E-1 was a fighter-bomber and exploded upon impact.

54. Some of the exploded 7.92mm machine-gun rounds discovered at Pollach's crash-site.

55. An Me 109E fighter-bomber (Jagadbomber or 'Jabo' in German) similar to Pollach's.

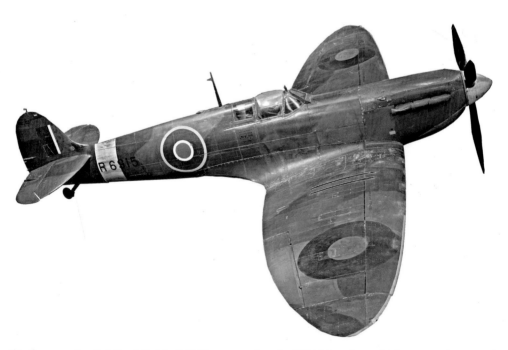

56. Supermarine Spitfire Mk IA, R6915, preserved at the IWM London, which was on charge with 609 Squadron during the Battle of Britain, and in which Flying Officer Dundas, and Pilot Officers Agazarian, Miller and Ostazewski, all of whom are mentioned in this book, achieved aerial victories flying this machine.

bombers yet. The whole formation had already passed over London from the East, dropped its bombs and was now running for the coast as hard as it could, being harassed and worried the whole way by our Hurricanes and Spitfires.

We were too low to attack it and started to climb and a terrific chase took place all the way down to Brighton.

But we had too much leeway to be made up over such a short distance and they crossed the coast before we managed to get into range, though a number were shot down by other squadrons.

I saw one Hurricane pilot, whose machine had been hit, jump out and open his parachute. Immediately, four other Hurricanes made straight for him and circled round and round till he reached the ground, watching carefully to see that no enemy fighter shot him in mid-air.

On September 13th, I got four days' leave, and accordingly packed my things and prepared to get away at midday. Geoff and Michael had just come back from 24 hours in London and I had a chat with them before leaving. Geoff and I made the usual arrangement that we always made when either of us got leave – that the one who went away would ring the other one's people when he got home and tell them that everything was ok.

Forshaw and I got into the Magister and started it up, and Geoff, having bade me give his love to D., waved goodbye and wandered down to his Spitfire with Michael to check it over.

My last glimpse of him was very typical – in high spirits after an amusing day with Michael, full of zest and appreciation of life, and looking as fit and pink and massive as he always did.

Together we had had a grand few weeks of successful flying and fighting, sleeping in deckchairs in the sun, playing our rough game of cricket, and spending the usual amusing evenings at the Square Club in Andover. Geoff had entered into all this with his usual infectious enthusiasm and enjoyment, and I have never seen him so happy or in such excellent form. Certainly, he never had any premonition of death, and up to the very last moments of his life, I believe he was as happy, as carefree, and as gay as he always had been.

And thus, with a few casual remarks and jokes, I said goodbye to the person who, apart from the family, had been my closest friend for the whole of my life.

Forshaw and I took off in the Magister and flew to Peterborough, where I made a somewhat exciting landing in a very high wind and nearly tipped the poor little Magister up on its nose.

Forshaw then continued on his way to London, and I walked to the station, caught a train north and arrived home a few hours later. It was grand to be home again and Dorothy and I saw a lot of people and altogether enjoyed our time together very much indeed.

On Sunday morning, September 15th, we went up to Frank Hirst's for a beer before lunch. We arrived there at about 12.15 p.m.

At this moment, 200 miles away over Surrey, 609 were diving down to attack a very large enemy bomber formation, and Geoff was being shot down by some Messerschmitts.

But we could not know this at the time, and we spent a very pleasant hour there.

The following morning, I came into the house just before lunch and Mother told me that Mrs Gaunt had just rather rung her up to say that Geoff was reported Missing. I immediately wired to Michael asking for information and he replied saying that Geoff had not come back after a fight over London.

I think that the Gaunts and our family were still pinning a few last hopes on the word "Missing", but I knew perfectly well from previous experiences that this merely meant that the body and aircraft had not yet been found or any rate identified.

It was a stunning blow to all of us, and though the Berrys arrived that evening for Maurice's wedding, what would otherwise have been a very pleasant and happy evening was actually very depressing and sad.

I left home the following day and went up to London on my way back to Andover. I had not been in London since the real "Blitz" started and found everything changed very much.

By 8 p.m. very few people were to be seen in the West End, and the bars and restaurants were doing about one-tenth of their normal trade. However, I met a very amusing Canadian private and we had a few beers together. He had been in the First Canadian Division who landed at Le Havre towards the end of the battle in France. They were embarked again almost immediately and had to leave all their equipment – tanks, guns, stores, etc on the quay. He and a few friends, however, had wandered up into the town, which was practically deserted and found a pub where they put their bayonets into a cask of wine and by the time the boat sailed again, they were completely drunk, and were left behind.

So, they made their way down to Bordeaux and were able to get a boat there. He spent a fortnight in Bournemouth on his return and then reported back to his unit and was given 14 days C.B. (confined to barracks) which he thought very satisfactory considering the good time he had had!

I said goodbye to my Canadian friend at about 11 p.m. and walked back to the hotel through practically deserted streets. I could hear one or two German machines quite plainly and the guns were firing at them rather spasmodically but the whole business was not nearly as spectacular or as noisy as I had been led to believe. I went to bed and slept soundly, despite the fact that John Lewis and various other stores in Oxford Street were hit that night.

Next morning after a good night's sleep, bath and shave, I bounced down to breakfast in grand form, to find everybody coming up from the shelters looking rather bleary eyed and dishevelled after a sleepless night. I felt rather guilty!

And so back to Wallop, to hear all the known details of Geoff's death.

On September 15th, the day of his death, there had occurred the biggest enemy raids yet experienced, and in terrific battles over

London and the South East, 185 raiders had been definitely destroyed, besides many more probables and damaged. The R.A.F. losses were about 28 fighters, but only 12 pilots – Geoff had been one of these.

The squadron had taken off from Wallop about 11.30 a.m. and flown up to West London. They were then ordered South East and at 12.15 p.m. they met a very big bomber formation at nearly 20,000 feet over Kenley (just south of Croydon). 609 attacked immediately.

Geoff was one of a section of four machines led by Michael, with Geoff No. 2 and two others behind him.

Michael led the section in against the bombers but could give only a short burst of fire because a lot of Messerschmitts were coming up from the rear to protect the bombers. So, Michael broke away very quickly and the last two pilots in the section, John Curchin and Shorty (the American) did not even have time to fire but dived away immediately.

They last saw Geoff following Michael into the attack, and after that he was never seen alive again. He had either been hit by one of the rear gunners in the bombers (Michael came under very heavy fire from them) or more probably, in his intense desire to destroy a bomber, he stayed too long firing at them and was destroyed by the Me. 110s from behind.

Apart from this accident, 609 had quite a good day and destroyed several enemy aircraft. Ogilvie, a Canadian, chased a Dornier across London and shot it down near Victoria Station. Incidentally, the Queen of Holland saw this action from her bedroom window and sent a letter of congratulations through her A.D.C. (Aide-de-Camp) to Ogilvie.

The squadron were in action again in the afternoon and caught two Dorniers over the Channel that had dropped behind the rest of the enemy formation.

Michael was again leading Green Section and ordered them to follow him into the attack. He then discovered that they had all left him already and had dived down to attack without orders. So, instead of leading the movement, he arrived last of all!

The two wretched Dorniers were absolutely overwhelmed by the 12 Spitfires and were literally shot to pieces in mid-air.

For four days after Geoff's death we heard absolutely no details of the crash or anything. However, on the Thursday, the R.A.F. at Kenley wired to say that his body and Spitfire had been found near there. The crash had been seen by a number of people but the machine, having fallen for about 20,000 feet, was absolutely smashed and impossible to identify by any number or letter. Geoff's body was also pretty badly battered, and, in the end, they identified him only by the name in his collar band. He had made no attempt to escape from the machine, though in such a long dive he would have had ample time, had he been alive.

The funeral took place at Huddersfield on September 26th, and I flew up home in order to be present and also to represent the squadron. Unfortunately, however, the Magister had something wrong with one wheel and though one or two men worked nobly to get it right in time, I was rather late in starting. I landed at Yeadon and then raced over to Huddersfield by car and arrived at the church about 15 minutes after the service was finished. Everybody had gone.

The grave was still open. I walked over to it and stood there for a moment, looking at the inscription on the coffin of this very gallant and delightful friend.

We had known each other all our lives and been at school together for about twelve years and after that we were in the same squadron. He was so much liked by our family, and spent so much time with us that really, he was rather like another brother to Paul and me. He possessed a most attractive and vital personality, and entered into everything with the utmost keenness and zest; I don't think I have ever known anybody who appeared generally to derive as much enjoyment from life. And what grand times we have had together – the gay evenings we used to enjoy before the war, those glorious summer days we spent rock climbing on Scafell and Doe Crag, or sailing unskilfully but with endless amusement in a dinghy on Windermere.

And then, during this last summer, the happy days we spent at Wallop, fighting together, having our practice dogfights together, playing tip and run, and going into Salisbury or Andover every evening with the rest of the squadron. The memories which I shall always have of Geoff will be those of happiness, and laughter and gaiety.

Only a week or two before his death, I said to him one evening that if anything were ever to happen to him, I should feel rather responsible because he was an only son, and I had persuaded him to join the R.A.F. with me. He replied that he would always be grateful to me for my persuasion because the year that he had spent in the R.A.F. since the beginning of the war had been the best year of his life, and he wouldn't have gone into the Army for anything and missed all this glorious fun.

Looking back, I don't think that his death was altogether a surprise to me, because for some time past I had the feeling that he would not survive this war. I had the same feeling about some other friends, notably Basil Fisher and Gordon Mitchell, and when we were at Peebles, two months before Gordon's death, I told D. that I was sure he would be killed, and she reminded me of this remark soon after she heard of his death.

On the other hand, I am firmly convinced that some other people – Michael for instance – will not be killed. I cannot explain this feeling, it is not based on their qualities as pilots because they were all good pilots, and Geoff particularly so, even though he hadn't much experience of air fighting. But none of us had to start with.

The other fact that impressed me about Geoff's death (and one or two other deaths that occurred soon after) was that they seemed to have no effect on the squadron's spirit and this was a great contrast to the feeling after the casualties at Dunkirk and Weymouth a month or two before. Everybody was naturally very shocked, because Geoff had been so popular, but we were now so consistently successful and strong in our confidence that we had the enemy "just where we wanted him" that nobody was shaken in the least.

But for me it was the biggest loss that I had ever experienced.

I left the churchyard and went down home. We spent the rest of the day very quietly and D. and I went for a walk in the afternoon, and then I went up to see the Gaunts and gave them some photographs of Geoff that I had.

They were being very brave about it all, but it was an absolutely overwhelming blow to them because he was their only son. It reminded me only too well of Gordon Mitchell's death – another only son.

Geoff, Gordon and I were always very pleased to reflect that three Old Leysians should be together in the same squadron. But I was the only one left.

The following morning Father drove me over to Yeadon and I took off in the Magister to return to Wallop.

I had a pleasant journey down and flew via Little Rissington and Bourton on the Water. It was all looking as peaceful and sleepy as ever, and I could see the New Inn, where we had spent the whole winter, and the village street, and Hartwells garage and the Windrush flowing gently through it all. I could even see the orange curtains in our bedroom!

How much had happened since we were all there together! It was only just over four months since we left, and yet it seemed like an age, because so much had happened in that time.

I got back to Wallop to find that I had missed a lot of excitement the previous day. A very big daylight raid had penetrated to Bristol and bombed the Bristol Aeroplane Company, doing quite a lot of damage, though none of it very vital. 609 had been heavily engaged and again got quite a good score – about six confirmed, with no losses.

A running fight had been taking place from Weymouth, where they crossed the coast, all up through Somerset to Bristol and then back again. A number of our squadrons were engaged and the Germans suffered fairly heavy losses, though I think on the whole they could claim it as a fairly satisfactory raid.

Shortly after my return, a raid came into Southampton and we took off to intercept it. This was not a very satisfactory action for us – just before we attacked the bombers, a lot of Me. 109s dived on us from out of the sun and we were split up.

We suffered no casualties, and the German pilots can't have been very good – had the positions been reversed and we had dived on them in similar circumstances a lot of them would never have seen the Fatherland again.

In the rather confused action which ensued, some of us did not find a target (I was one!) and had to return without firing a round.

However, some people, including the C.O., did better and we again scored five or six without loss.

Unfortunately, the following day Mac had to go to hospital with ear trouble and the doctors told him that he would not be able to go above 5,000 feet in future. This meant of course that he could not remain in a fighter squadron and poor Mac was very sad about it.

So were we all – he had been a grand chap and an excellent Flight Commander, besides being very successful individually. I am glad to say that he got the D.F.C. a few days later which bucked him up a lot.

He was the third case of ear trouble that we had in two months. High altitude flying and fighting imposes a very great strain on the ears owing to the rapid changes of pressure when diving from big heights. One day in a flight at nearly 25,000 feet, Mac's oxygen failed and he lost consciousness almost immediately and woke up again to find he was doing a screaming dive at well over 400 m.p.h. and very near to the ground. He managed to pull out just in time, but he had dived nearly five miles in a few seconds, and it was this incident which ruined his ears.

On Friday, September 27th, another big raid tried to get through to Bristol and we took off from Wallop to intercept. The orders for us to go had come through rather late, and when we sighted the bombers, we were too far behind to be able to catch them (they were very well taken care of by other squadrons however).

Also, the C.O. had a bad cold and the height caused him such agony in his ears that he had to drop out – he was off flying for over a week as a result of this effort.

Anyway, we continued our patrol and soon after we saw a squadron of Me. 110s circling over Swanage at 25,000 feet, waiting to protect their bombers on their return. We immediately turned towards the enemy fighters and started to climb above them.

They had formed one of their defensive circles, going round and round on each other's tails – altogether quite a tough nut to crack. Incidentally, this was the first time in this war that we had met the enemy on even terms. Generally, we were outnumbered by anything from 3 to 1 up to 10 to 1. But on this glorious occasion there were 15 of them and 12 of us and we made the most of it!

We were very close to them now and we started to dive. I think these moments just before the clash are the most gloriously exciting moments of my life. You sit there behind a great engine that seems as vibrant and alive as you are yourself, your thumb waits expectantly on the trigger, and your eyes watch the gun sights through which in a few seconds an enemy will be flying in a veritable hail of fire.

And all around you, in front and behind, there are your friends too, all eager and excited, all thundering down together into the attack! The memory of such moments is burnt into my mind for ever.

I was flying just behind Miller and he turned slightly left to attack an Me. 110 which was coming towards him. But the German was as determined as Miller, and refused to give way or alter course to avoid this head-on attack. Their aggregate speed of closing was at least 600 m.p.h. and an instant later they collided.

There was a terrific explosion and a sheet of flame seemed to hang in the air like a great ball of fire. Many little shattered fragments fluttered down and that was all.

Miller was killed instantly and so were his two German opponents and hardly any trace of them was ever found.

Poor old Mick – he was a pleasant fellow and I had known him for a year as he was at Rissington with me. His brother, also in the R.A.F., was killed only two months before in a raid on Germany.

All this happened in an instant, and I turned right in order to get onto the tail of a Hun. My Spitfire immediately went into a very vicious right-hand spin – the atmosphere at these great altitudes is so rarefied that machines are very much more difficult to manoeuvre – and when I recovered, I had lost my German.

The whole enemy circle had been broken up by our attack, and various Messerschmitts were streaming out to sea with our people chasing after them.

I saw an Me. 110 about half a mile ahead and went after him on full throttle. He also was going flat out and diving slightly to get extra speed, but my beloved Spitfire rose nobly to the occasion and worked up to over 400 m.p.h. and I caught him fairly easily, though we were about 20 miles out to sea by this time.

The enemy rear gunner, who obviously had wind up, opened fire at me at hopelessly long range, though I could see his tracer bullets flicking past me.

I dived slightly to get underneath his tail as he could not fire at me in that position, and when in range I opened fire. I must have killed the gunner because he never fired again, though I must have been visible to him at times, and at very close range. I put all my ammunition into the fuselage and port engine and the latter started to smoke furiously. To my intense disgust my ammunition ran out before he went down and I thought that I might have to let him go after all, badly damaged though he was.

But at this moment a voice said on the R.T. "Ok. Ok. Help coming" and Bisdee gradually overtook us and finished off the Me. which fell into the sea. "Bishop" and I were credited with one half each in this affair.

Apart from Mick's death the whole fight had been a great success, and six Huns were destroyed and there were one or two more probables. I bet that German squadron doesn't look forward to their next trip over England – I know what we should feel like if we were attacked by an equal number of Messerschmitts and half our squadron was destroyed in four minutes. [See Appendix III]

It's a very good thing to instil into the Hun a healthy respect for the R.A.F.

The following day was rather cloudy and nothing very much happened except that Wallop was bombed by a single Ju. 88 which came over under cover of cloud. Some Hurricanes were up after him and one of them sighted him when about five miles south of the aerodrome. A terrific chase ensued with the Hun dodging in and out of the cloud and the Hurricane firing madly at him wherever he could see him.

They passed right over our heads at about 1,000 feet; I had never heard a fighter's eight machine-guns firing before, except when in the cockpit myself when the noise is very muffled, and I was amazed! It's the most terrific tearing, ripping sound just like hundreds of girls ripping up sheets of calico. I must say this Hun pilot was very cool because despite the Hurricane on his tail he still did his run-up towards his target and let go four big bombs which fell just beyond our mess, made four huge craters in a field, shook everybody in the mess, but did no damage whatsoever. A very lucky escape.

Novi got so excited when the Hurricane started firing that he jumped up on to some sandbags and shouted at the top of his voice to the Hurricane "Shoot, shoot"! The Junkers got back into cloud again before the Hurricane could shoot him down, but he had to land about 20 miles away as one of the Hurricane's bullets had hit an oil pipe. So, we got him after all.

Just about this time, Michael made a joke which I think is worth recording.

All of us pilot officers are not exactly overpaid for our services and Michael composed the following variation of Mr. Churchill's now famous phrase – "Never in the history of human conflict has so much been owed by so many to so few – for so little"!

Monday, September 30th, was a very eventful day for me and easily the most successful that I had experienced.

The weather was brilliantly clear and when we got up, we shook our heads dismally as we knew there would be a lot of trouble!

We arrived down at dispersal point about 7.30 a.m., and I walked over to my Spitfire, as I always did first thing every morning, and checked over everything in the cockpit with the utmost care because if we got any orders to "scramble" later, we always had to get off the ground in such a hurry that one had no time to look at anything.

So I checked over the whole machine with great care, looked at the petrol gauges and turned on the petrol, checked that the mixture control was in "Rich" and the airscrew in fine pitch, set the elevator trim, opened the radiator, turned on the oxygen and checked it, switched on the reflector sights, checked the air pressure for the gun system, and switched on the camera gun. Everything was perfect, as indeed it always was. I walked back to the hut, put on my Mae West and started to write up this diary – my daily occupation.

All the rest of the squadron who happened to be on duty were down there too – twelve of us in all, some writing or reading, some asleep, and the rest playing cards.

Soon after 10.30 a.m. we heard the telephone bell ring in the next room, and the telephone orderly ran to our door and yelled in his usual stentorian voice "Squadron scramble, patrol Swanage, Angels 25" (the latter meaning 25,000 feet).

I threw this diary into a chair; the card players dropped their hands and everybody sprinted out of the door towards their machines. All the mechanics were running hard too, and by the time I got to my Spitfire, two men were already there to help me on with my parachute and then fasten my harness when I was in the cockpit. I put on the starter and ignition switches, turned on the R.T., gave the priming pump a couple of strokes and pressed the starter button. The engine started immediately, and I put on my helmet and oxygen mask, turned on the oxygen and within ninety seconds of the alarm coming through, we were all taxying out on the aerodrome.

I was leading Green Section with Novi and John Curchin behind me, and we got out to our taking off point and turned into wind. I looked round at Novi, and he gave me "Thumbs Up", meaning all ok, and Johnny did likewise.

I dropped my hand, opened the throttle and we all accelerated rapidly over the aerodrome and took off. The rest of the squadron were either taking off or already in the air and we all joined up and started to climb towards Swanage, nearly 50 miles away.

I used to love flying with the squadron like this – it was always a grand sight to see twelve Spitfires sweeping along together in formation – twelve pilots, fifteen thousand horsepower, and 96 machine-guns with a total fire power of 120,000 rounds a minute. Altogether quite a formidable proposition.

A few moments later the Controller in the Operations Room at Middle Wallop called us on the R.T. "Hallo, Sorbo Leader, (Sorbo was our call sign) more than 100 enemy aircraft now approaching Swanage, Angels 20". The C.O. replied immediately, "Sorbo Leader answering Bandy (Middle Wallop) your message received and understood".

We continued to climb – 10,000 feet – 15,000 – 20,000 – 25,000 feet – and as we got higher, I kept turning on more and more oxygen for myself and every few moments looking at the dashboard to check the oil pressure and temperature, radiator temperature, boost pressure, and oxygen delivery. Everything was running like clockwork – always very reassuring when you know that a big fight is imminent.

We were now high over Dorset – nearly 27,000 feet, and rapidly approaching Swanage, when somebody called up on the R.T. "Enemy ahead on the left". I looked round and saw, a long way in the distance, a big formation of enemy fighters circling over the coast. I don't think there were any bombers on this occasion – it was just a very strong fighter patrol sent over to annoy us and destroy as many of our fighters as possible.

Howell (who was leading us that day as the C.O. was ill) altered direction slightly and we flew right into Weymouth Bay and then turned in towards land again, so as to approach the enemy from the sun. This was a clever move as it turned out.

It was obviously now a matter of only moments before we were in the thick of it, and I switched on my reflector sights, turned my trigger onto "Fire", put the airscrew into fine pitch, and pushed the small handle on the throttle quadrant that allows one to use emergency full power.

Gosh, those are exciting moments!

A few seconds later, about six Me. 109s flew across right in front of us – I don't think they saw us till too late as we were coming out of the sun. Michael was leading Blue section and I was leading Green, and immediately we swung our sections round and turned onto the tails of the enemy. They then saw us – too late – and tried to escape by diving.

We all went down after them in one glorious rush, and I saw Michael who was about 100 yards ahead of me, open fire at the last Messerschmitt in the enemy line. A few seconds later, this machine more or less fell to pieces in mid-air, some very nice shooting on Michael's part! I distinctly remember him saying on the R.T. "That's got you, you bastard", though he never recollects it!

The victim that I had selected for myself was about 500 yards ahead of me and still diving hard at very high speed. Gosh, what a dive that was!

I came down on full throttle from 27,000 feet to 1,000 feet in a matter of a few seconds, and the speed rose with incredible swiftness – 400 m.p.h. – 500 – 550 – 600 m.p.h. I had never reached this speed before and probably never shall again.

I have a sort of dim recollection of the sea coming up towards me at an incredible rate and also feeling an awful pain in my ears, though I was not really conscious of this in the heat of the moment. I pulled out of the dive as gently as I could, but the strain was terrific and there was a sort of black mist in front of my eyes, though I did not quite "black-out".

The Messerschmitt was now just ahead of me.

I came up behind him and slightly below and gave him a terrific burst of fire at very close range. The effect of a Spitfire's eight guns has to be seen to be believed. Hundreds of bullets poured into him and he rocked violently, then turned over on his back, burst into flames and dived straight down into the sea a few miles off Swanage. The pilot made no attempt to get out and was obviously dead.

I watched him hit the water in a great cloud of white foam, and then turned round to see what was going on.

Various of our Spitfires were chasing Messerschmitts all over the place and obviously a very nice little massacre was in progress, as a few seconds later I saw another Hun go into the sea. I then saw another Me. 109 going back to France as hard as he could, and I chased after him, caught him fairly easily and put a good burst into him. He swerved slightly, his cockpit covering broke off the machine and flew past my head and he then dived steeply.

I waited to see him hit the water but he was only shamming as he flattened out again just above the sea, and continued full speed for home though his machine was now smoking and obviously badly hit.

For the first time in this war, I felt a certain pity for this German pilot and was rather reluctant to finish him off. From the moment I saw him, he really had no chance of escape as my Spitfire was so much faster than his Messerschmitt, and the last few moments must have been absolute hell for him.

But if I let him go, he would come back to England another day and possibly shoot down some of our pilots. In the few seconds during which all this was happening I did not consciously make these reflections – my blood was up anyway, and I was very excited, but I distinctly remember feeling rather reluctant.

However, I caught him up again and made no mistake this time. I fired almost all my remaining ammunition at very close range, and he crashed into the sea, going at terrific speed, and disappeared immediately. I circled round the spot but there was no trace of anything.

I now looked round and discovered that I could see the French coast very clearly ahead and that I was only 20 miles from Cherbourg.

England was nowhere to be seen!

In the excitement of the chase, I had not realised how far we were going, and I turned round very hastily and started on my 60-mile trip back to the English coast, but it seemed to take a long time and I was very relieved when, still a long way out to sea, I saw the white cliffs begin to appear ahead. One never knows what an engine may do after running it so long on absolutely full throttle and the idea of drowning out in mid-Channel never did appeal to me!

I was now feeling very happy and pleased with myself – I had always wanted to get two Huns in one fight. I approached the cliffs in Weymouth Bay, flying only a few feet over the water at nearly 300 m.p.h. and when I was almost hitting the cliff, I pulled the stick back and rocketed over the top, to the very considerable amazement of some soldiers who were on the other side. And so back to Wallop, flying very low the whole way, generally playing the fool and feeling gloriously happy and elated!

Everybody was safely back and we had destroyed five Messerschmitts – quite a nice morning's work.

In the afternoon there was another alarm at about 3.30 p.m., and again we took off and made for the coast at Swanage, climbing all the time. We passed over Warmwell and then turned round and approached Swanage down from the sun.

A few moments later we saw a few machines down on our left, which I thought were Hurricanes. However, Howell who was leading the squadron, told me to take Green Section down to investigate. So, three of us, Novi, John Curchin and I, broke away from the squadron and dived down to the left. Unfortunately, Curchin's engine was giving trouble and he could not keep up with Novi and me, and got left a long way behind.

I was still under the impression that these machines were Hurricanes but as we got nearer, I recognised them as Me. 109s and shouted to Novi accordingly.

We both attacked together, and he opened fire on the last one on the line and shot it down almost immediately – I don't think they ever saw us till we opened fire as we dived on them out of the sun.

They split up quickly and I went after one and gave him a quick deflection burst which I don't think hit him, but certainly startled him as he promptly proceeded to take the most violent evasive tactics. For nearly two minutes we dived and zoomed and turned madly all over the sky in a desperate effort to get on each other's tails. It was just like the practice dogfights that Geoff and I used to have together at Wallop, except that in this case the slightest mistake would probably cost the loser his life, instead of a pint of beer.

But the Spitfire is more manoeuvrable than the Messerschmitt, and I had no difficulty in keeping on his tail more or less, though he was sufficiently quick in his turns to prevent me getting my sights on him for more than a fraction of a second.

Finally, after a dive even faster than before, he zoomed up almost vertically into the sun, hoping to shake me off that way. Almost completely dazzled, I managed nevertheless to follow him up and when he did a stall turn at the top, I got another quick burst at him without apparent effect.

This was the most enjoyable scrap I had ever had and it was grand to feel that the advantages were even and it was just my skill and quickness against his, and with nobody else to worry about.

In all the previous fights, it had just been a case of catching somebody by virtue of the Spitfire's great speed, and then simply blasting them with eight guns, all the time wondering who the hell may be coming up behind you to give you "hot pants" (as our Americans used to say!).

Anyway, he dived down into a layer of cloud below and I chased after him, missed him with another burst, and then chased through this cloud for some miles, dodging in and out and seeing him for a fleeting instant every now and then.

He wasn't very clever about this, as he never changed course in the cloud and thus if I lost him, I had only to keep straight on and I would pick him up again.

We shot over Weymouth going very fast indeed, and passed out to sea. This was his undoing, as he probably thought he had shaken me off and he made the bad mistake of climbing out of the cloud. I climbed up behind, came into very close range and then absolutely blasted him. He turned over, and spun down into the cloud, streaming glycol smoke, which meant that his radiator had been hit.

I dived below cloud, but could see no trace of him at all, and I think there can be very little doubt that he crashed into the sea, as he was badly hit and certainly could not have reached France with a radiator leaking like that. But I had not seen him actually crash and therefore could only claim him as a "Probable".

I hung around for a few minutes but saw no other Huns and returned to Wallop. The rest of the squadron had not been in action and so Novi and I were the only lucky ones. He had shot down two of the Me. 109s and the pilot got out of the second machine and tried to open his parachute.

One of the rigging lines fouled it however, and it only opened slightly, and the unfortunate German therefore continued his drop with scarcely any reduction in speed and was killed.

Novi, bloodthirsty as ever where Germans are concerned, recounted this story to us with great relish and a wealth of very descriptive gestures!

This had been a very good day for B Flight, and we all felt in very good form that evening and Michael, Aggy, John Curchin and

I went over to Winchester and met Major and Mrs Berry and Pam and Maurice – the first time I'd seen them since their wedding. We all had a very pleasant and amusing evening together.

And thus ended that eventful month, September 1940.

October 1940

In the first few days of October, to our very real regret, the news came through that the C.O. was leaving us. He had been promoted Wing Commander and was going to command the R.A.F. station at Exeter.

We were all very sorry indeed to lose him. He came to us when we were not a particularly successful squadron; he held everybody together by his magnificent example in the bad days when we had so many tragic losses without any victories, and he trained us so thoroughly and led us so skilfully that we were one of the finest fighter squadrons in the R.A.F. when he left. As Air Vice-Marshal Sir Quintin Brand (commanding No.10 Fighter Group) said a few weeks later, whenever he heard that 609 were going into action, he always knew that plenty of Huns would be destroyed, at very little or no cost to us.

Certainly the C.O. had done very well indeed, and we were all delighted to hear, just before he left, that he had been awarded the D.S.O.

We all expected that Frank Howell, "A" Flight's commander, would take command of the Squadron and certainly it would have been a very good thing, because in the C.O.'s absence he always led us so well that everybody had complete confidence in him.

However, the powers that be decreed otherwise, and we got instead Squadron Leader Robinson who proved to be a very sound pilot and leader. He was the pilot who, about two months before, shot down two Me. 109s and having finished his ammunition, saw a third 109, and chased it for 40 miles and finally so frightened the German pilot by making dummy attacks at him, that he landed in a field and was captured! The C.O. then threw him a packet of Players, waved and the German waved back and then he flew off. Altogether a very cool bit of work.

We had a terrific farewell party the night before the C.O. left. Pamela and Maurice came over for the early part of the evening and we all adjourned to the Square Club. We then came back for dinner at Wallop and went down to the C.O.'s house, where a large barrel of beer had been specially installed for the occasion and a very gay and rather rowdy time was had by all.

The next morning the C.O. came down to dispersal point where we all were, and bade us all goodbye and good luck, and said how proud he had been to command such a grand squadron. He stood there looking exactly like a rather sheepish schoolboy, while we all sang "For he's a jolly good fellow" at the tops of our voices and then he drove off, en route for Exeter.

What a grand C.O. we were losing!

That afternoon we took off to do some practice flying and when we came in to land again, and put our undercarriages down, only one of Novi's wheels would come down and the other remained locked obstinately in the raised position. Try as he could, he was unable to move it and this meant that it was very dangerous to land as one wheel would hit the ground and the Spitfire – still doing about 74 m.p.h. – would then somersault towards the missing wheel. I called him up on the R.T. and told him that he must not land but instead climb up and escape by parachute.

I was flying very close to him and we climbed up to 5,000 feet over Salisbury Plain, and then Novi opened his sliding hood, took of his helmet, undid his harness and prepared to abandon ship. However, he seemed to experience some difficulty in getting out of the cockpit into the slipstream, and finally he turned the machine over on to its back, and dropped neatly out of his seat!

The Spitfire promptly dived into the corner of a small wood and burst into a sheet of flame, while Novi, after fumbling for his release cord, opened his parachute and a few minutes later dropped into the middle of a hen run, to the consternation of the poultry.

People seemed to spring up from all over the place and rush towards him and so I circled the spot for a few moments as I thought that with his rather broken English he might be mistaken for a German parachutist. But everything was ok, we sent out a car to collect him, and half an hour later he was in the mess again, none the worse for his experience except for a bruised arm.

The machine that he had been flying was not a very good one – it was rather old and slower than the new ones, so we were all very grateful to him for writing it off!

The following day, October 6th, was very misty and rainy and we did not even go down to dispersal point, but sat in the mess, and read the papers and had a beer before lunch. The weather seemed so thick that obviously no Hun would get over – or so we thought!

However, at about 12.30 p.m. the loudspeaker announced that an enemy aircraft was approaching Wallop in the clouds. We could do nothing about it as we could not possibly take off in such weather, so we ordered another beer apiece and were rather amused by the whole business.

A few seconds later, we all heard a very sharp whistle and everybody in the mess – about 30 people in all, lounging in armchairs and reading the papers – suddenly threw themselves with astonishing agility onto the floor. I remember that Michael and I met with a crash under the table and spilt all the beer, while our Intelligence Officer, McKay, who is too fat to get underneath anything, merely lay hopefully on his back.

There were two big flashes outside the window, and two terrific explosions that seemed to rock the whole building to its foundations. We cowered and waited expectantly for the next. But nothing happened, and we rose cautiously to our feet.

No windows were broken (except one in the Billiard Room where John Curchin was just playing a shot as the bomb dropped, and he was so surprised that he slung his cue through the window) and really no damage had been done.

The bombs had fallen in a field just in front of the mess and whether the German had just dropped them at random or whether he located Wallop by means of a directional beam, I don't know. If he really intended them for us then it was pretty good shooting, considering the appalling weather. We walked over to inspect the craters, picked up a few splinters and wandered back and ordered a final glass of beer before lunch, to replace those spilt in the rapid dive onto the floor!

The following day, Monday, October 7th, dawned very bright and clear, and we expected trouble from the moment we got up.

But nothing happened till about 3.30 p.m. when we were ordered off to patrol Weymouth at a height of 25,000 feet. We took off and climbed up steadily in a south-westerly direction, trying to get as much height as possible before reaching the coast.

I don't think I have ever seen such a clear day in my life. From 15,000 feet I could see Plymouth and far beyond into Devon and Cornwall, and the whole of the coast of South Wales, from the Severn to Gloucester, all down past Newport and Cardiff, and right along beyond Swansea towards the West. And on our left, towards the south, the Channel glistened and sparkled in the sun and the French coast and the Channel Islands, although 75 miles away, seemed to be just under my wing tip.

But I can't say that I appreciated this superb view very much under the circumstances, because I was busily engaged in weaving to and fro behind the squadron anxiously scanning the sky for the Messerschmitts which we knew would soon be arriving.

The sun was so brilliant and dazzling that it was very difficult to see anything clearly in the glare, and yet this made it even more important to maintain the utmost vigilance, as the Me. 109s are very good at jumping on one out of the sun.

When we were almost at Weymouth and at about 20,000 feet, we saw an enemy bomber formation some miles out to sea, and at the same moment various people saw a lot of Me. 109s above us, apparently about to dive down and attack us. About four people at once started to shout warnings on the R.T. and there was a perfect babel of excited voices, which rather added to the confusion.

B Flight was rather behind A Flight and we started to break up, as it's quite hopeless to watch enemy aircraft above and behind, and at the same time keep in formation with the rest of the squadron.

I hardly saw anybody again for the rest of the action, and most of us never engaged at all. Several of us continued to patrol over Weymouth for about half an hour, by which time the whole affair was obviously over, and Operations Room told us to land.

When we got back to Wallop, we found that A Flight had been rather more successful. Being in front of us and therefore to some extent guarded by us, they managed to keep together and attacked a formation of Me. 110s and destroyed five or six of them.

We now had a very anxious half hour, as four pilots were still missing. However, some news soon started to come through.

John Dundas's machine had been hit by a cannon shell from an Me. 110 which came up behind him as he was engaged in shooting down an Me. 109. The shell burst in the wing, and put a lot of little splinters into his side but he wasn't badly hurt and landed at Warmwell, and returned to Wallop the next day.

Michael Staples got a bullet in his leg and baled out and landed near Blandford where they took him to hospital. He was ok, though, with a rather big hole in his leg.

Frank Howell shot down an Me. 110 in flames near Shaftesbury, but the rear-gunner managed to hit Frank's engine and he had to land in a field near Shaftesbury.

Within two minutes, a crowd of people had sprung up from an apparently deserted countryside, and offered him cups of tea and coffee. The police and soldiers then arrived on the scene and had a great argument as to who should give him a party that night. The police won, and bore Frank off in triumph to the local pub where the police force and the inhabitants plied him (and themselves) with pints of beer for four solid hours and then drove him back to Wallop and delivered him into the mess in a distinctly intoxicated condition!

Well that was three out of four safe, but Sergeant Feary was still missing. We waited for some hours, hoping to hear that he had landed somewhere, but later that evening, Warmwell rang up to say that his body had been found near there. He was last seen by us when attacking the Me. 110s, and his machine must have been hit because a number of men at Warmwell saw his Spitfire spinning down from a great height.

He recovered from the spin, got into another one, recovered again, spun again and then apparently decided to get out. But he had left it too late because his parachute did not have time to open properly and he was killed by the fall. He had not been hit at all and if only he hadn't stayed so long in the damaged machine, he would have almost certainly been quite ok.

A great pity as he was a very good and resolute pilot and had been all through the summer's fighting.

By a very tragic coincidence, on the afternoon that this paragraph was written – November 28th – both John Dundas and Paul Baillon were killed over the Isle of Wight, during a raid into Southampton.

The last heard of Dundas was when he called up on the R.T. and said that he had shot down an Me. 109. He never came back and a few days later the German official communiqué said that one of their most successful fighter pilots – Major Wick – had been shot down by an English fighter near the Isle of Wight and that the English machine itself was immediately shot down by another member of the German formation. As no English pilots claimed any victims in this fight, Major Wick must have been the Messerschmitt pilot that Dundas spoke about on the R.T.

Baillon also just disappeared. Two months later in January, Berlin sent a telegram to the Air Ministry saying that his body had been washed ashore at Boulogne and buried there.

Warmwell certainly seemed to be an unlucky spot for 609. Apart from the Dunkirk casualties, we lost eight pilots during the summer and seven of these – Peter Drummond-Hay, Pip Barran, Gordon Mitchell, Buchanan, Goodwin, Mick Miller and Sergeant Feary – were all killed within a few miles of Warmwell and Weymouth. Only Geoff Gaunt was killed near London, and when one considers how much fighting we did both in London and Southampton areas, it does seem curious that all our losses should occur near Weymouth.

A few days later I got five days leave and again flew to Peterborough and caught the train north from there.

D. and I spent a very pleasant few days at home and went to Betty and Arthur's wedding on the day before I returned. As usual I caught the afternoon train from Wakefield and arrived in London nearly two hours late as there was a big raid in progress. It was almost impossible to get a taxi at Kings Cross but finally about six of us crowded into one, and drove through the dark and deserted streets to Piccadilly. There was a lot of gunfire, and every now and then the deep "Whoom" of a bursting bomb could be heard.

I walked round to the Trocadero and had some dinner and then met a very amusing Canadian soldier (I always seemed to meet Canadians on my evenings in town!) we had a few beers together and then decided that we could do with some bacon and eggs. It was just about midnight and we walked round to Lyons Corner House in Coventry Street and ordered our food. We had just started our meal when there was a terrific crash outside – all the glass in the windows fell in, and the whole building seemed to rock to its foundations.

I was amazed by the complete lack of any panic or confusion – most people just looked up for a moment and then resumed their conversation again.

A few minutes later we walked outside and found that a bomb had fallen just on the other side of the road next to the Prince of Wales Theatre. Very little structural damage had been done as it exploded in a small open space, but there was hardly a window left in the whole of Coventry Street.

The pavements were almost ankle deep in broken glass and a large squad of men were just assembling, to start the job of clearing it all up.

So a few minutes later, I bade my Canadian friend goodnight and went back to bed at the hotel. There was no further excitement that night!

When I got back to Wallop, I found that very little had happened in my absence and for the next few days life continued to be very quiet.

However, the weather improved slowly and a few days later we were sitting down at dispersal point when the order came through to scramble. We all got off the ground and started to climb towards the coast. At about 10,000 feet there was some cloud and as soon as we got above this, I looked round and above, and saw many thousands of feet above us at least 30 Me. 110s accompanied by a lot of Me. 109s.

At first, I thought they were our own fighters and called up the C.O. and suggested that they were the Hurricanes of 234 Squadron. The C.O. took one look and replied "No, their formation is much too good – they must be Huns!" And so they were, as I recognised them a moment later.

We were in a very vulnerable and hopeless position – a long way below them and outlined against the white cloud underneath us. However, we continued to climb in the hope of somehow managing to get in one attack, and all the time we watched the Messerschmitts like cats, as sooner or later they would obviously drop down on us. Altogether rather an unpleasant few minutes!

It was very difficult watching them, as they were almost in the sun and the glare was awful.

Suddenly I saw two Me. 109s just behind John Dundas's Spitfire. How they got there I don't know – I never saw them come down and nobody else did either. They must have dived very fast indeed, and they had just opened fire when I saw them – I remember distinctly their yellow noses and the white streaks caused by their cannon shells.

I immediately shouted on the R.T. "Look out, Messerschmitts, they're coming down". I have never seen the squadron break up so quickly – everybody turned sharply away in all directions and dived hard for the cloud. I went down with everybody else, pulled out after a few thousand feet and looked round. Apart from a few Spitfires dashing around, there was nothing to be seen. We all waited a little longer but met no more enemy and soon afterwards we were ordered to land. And so, a lot of rather disgruntled pilots returned to Wallop.

Nobody was missing and John Dundas was quite ok, though there were one or two bullet holes in his wings. Those Me. 109 pilots must have been bad shots – if any of us had fired at them in similar circumstances they wouldn't have got away.

And there was more good news – we had shot down a couple of Me. 109s though it seemed incredible when we were at such a disadvantage. When the squadron broke up and dived away, both Aggy and Novi stayed up there with the Me. 109s – a very reckless though daring thing to do, since they were in such a hopeless position. However, like some other audacious schemes, it worked.

Aggy was just turning round when a bullet crashed through his cockpit roof three inches above his head, and several more hit his machine. He whipped round and saw two 109s calmly flying away and not paying the slightest attention to him – perhaps they thought that they had shot him down. So he caught them up and shot down the rear one!

Novi was also attacked, but managed to shoot down another 109, which crashed near Bournemouth. When the machine was near the ground the pilot got out and just managed to open his parachute in time, but landed very heavily and lay on the ground, probably winded by the fall. Novi circled round and said afterwards, in his rather broken English: "I circle round, bloddy German lies down, he is dead, ok. But I look again, he is now sitting up – no bloddy good"! He was very disappointed – in his opinion the only good Germans are dead Germans.

After this little affair, the bad weather set in again and we did very little for the next few weeks. After the long strain of the summer and autumn, when we hardly ever got out in the evening as we were on duty till dark, the reaction now began to set in and we seemed to go out to parties nearly every night either to Andover or Salisbury.

Maurice and Pamela were stationed quite near us at Romsey and they used to come over and see us sometimes and we had some very amusing evenings together.

On Thursday, October 17th, after a very uneventful and rainy day we came into the mess for tea and I got a plate and settled down in a chair to read the paper. A few minutes later the C.O. came up to me and threw something on the paper with the remark, "Look what the post has just brought for you".

It was the D.F.C. ribbon!

I was so surprised that I just stared at it for a moment without grasping what it meant. I remember getting to my feet, still rather dazed, and being congratulated by various people.

Johnny Curchin had got one also, and he soon produced a needle and thread and sewed his on. I took mine to my batman to fix it on my tunic and then walked downstairs again feeling better than I'd ever felt before!

We all had the most terrific party that night and, I should imagine, consumed most of the mess stock of Pimms.

Altogether a very riotous evening!

In the action on October 7th, in which Sergeant Feary was killed and Mike Staples wounded, we had brought our score of Huns definitely destroyed to 99, and as we seemed to get some fight every few days it looked as though we should complete our century very quickly.

But unfortunately, the German Air Force did not seem very keen to offer themselves up for the slaughter, and so we waited impatiently for over a fortnight, hoping every day that our luck would change. No batsman, hovering on the edge of his century, was ever more keen than we were to see the 100 up! But after the murderous losses inflicted on them in the previous two months, the Germans had reduced their daylight bombing activity practically to nil, and nothing seemed to come our way.

However, on Monday, October 21st, our chance arrived. The day was cloudy – ideal conditions for single bombers to carry out hit-and-run raids, and about 12.30 p.m. a Junkers 88 appeared out of the clouds and bombed an aircraft factory at Brockworth, near Gloucester. He then turned south again towards the coast at Bournemouth on his way home, flying very low the whole way so as to escape detection by any of our fighters who might be above.

Two of our people – Frank Howell and Hill – were up after him and were waiting near the coast to try and intercept him on his way out. A few moments later, Operations Room at Wallop called them up on the R.T. and said "He should be near you now, flying very low".

A second later they saw him practically underneath – a very nice bit of work on the part of Operations Room.

They both dived down to attack and Howell went in first, opened fire at very close range and damaged an engine badly. It must have been a very exciting chase as the Ju. 88 was, at times, going down below the level of the trees in his desperate efforts to escape.

Howell then broke away and Hill opened fire and almost immediately the Ju. dived into a field. There was a terrific explosion, and the wreckage was scattered over four fields. All the crew were killed instantly.

And that was that. There was great rejoicing at Wallop when the news came through a few minutes later, and a very considerable party organised for that night.

About 6.30 p.m. we trooped into the writing room and there found a couple of waiters behind the bar, almost hidden by the large stock of champagne and brandy that had been installed for the occasion.

They weren't hidden for long!

And thus we celebrated our century.

A day or two later I flew over to St. Athans near Cardiff to pick up a little aeroplane belonging to the C.O. as he wanted to have it at Wallop. I flew over with Ogilvie in the Harvard and we landed at St. Athans and went over to the hangar where the Drone was kept. I was amazed when I saw it!

It is a tiny single seater aeroplane with a 10 h.p. Ford engine and when we started it up it sounded like a motorcycle.

I didn't see how I could possibly fly over 120 miles in it! Ogilvie went back in the Harvard, having made several very gloomy jokes about my chances of survival, and I took off in the Drone. Its top speed was about 45 m.p.h. and it had a very slow rate of climb so that if I saw a hill about two miles ahead, I had to start climbing immediately in order to get over the top.

Altogether a great change from a Spitfire!

I flew round Cardiff and then along the flat stretch of coast towards Newport and when the river became fairly narrow, I crossed over and skirted round the north of Bristol and then down over Warminster towards Middle Wallop. I hardly ever went above 200 feet and caused a great sensation as I floated gently over the countryside, past farms and villages where I could see everybody running out to look at this strange craft. It was a lovely day and I thoroughly enjoyed my gentle "stroll" over such grand country.

I remember that near Warminster I joined up with a large flock of starlings that were going my way and we all flew along together quite happily for some miles after which I throttled back a little and let them race on ahead! And coming along a road over the Plain I met a convoy of Army lorries, crowded with troops, all going in the same direction as me and approximately at the same speed, so I flew along with them and so close that I could have practically reached out and shaken hands with them. They were all highly amused and waved back hard!

I arrived safely at Wallop amid great hilarity and many ribald remarks. The trip had taken 3½ hours and I used 4½ gallons of petrol! I think it was one of the most enjoyable flights I ever had.

A day or two after this I went home on leave from October 24th-29th. We had a very pleasant, quiet time and D. and I went to see various people and altogether enjoyed the few days very much.

On the 29th, I returned to Wallop for the official Centenary Party – the other one apparently having been unofficial though nobody would have noticed it!

Quite a lot of people came down – Air Marshal Barrett, Sir Quintin Brand, Air Commodore Peake, who was the first C.O. of the squadron in the happy days at Yeadon before the war, and – to our intense pleasure – our old C.O., Wing Commander Darley D.S.O., came up from Exeter. Also, various Guards officers came up from Camberley and arrived just before dusk and Michael and I took off in a couple of Spitfires and did a little formation flying and a few upward rolls for their benefit.

And so on to the party. Very considerable quantities of champagne were consumed, we had an excellent dinner and some speeches including one from Darley which we all cheered till we were hoarse.

It was very fitting that he should be there – under his command we had come through the summer campaign of 1940 with as fine a record as any squadron in the R.A.F. and this dinner, besides celebrating our century, was also celebrating a very successful few months of fighting. [See Appendix IV]

Sir Quintin Brand also congratulated us.

Later on, the evening became a distinctly riotous one, and altogether it was a very good party.

Just about this time a very unusual occurrence took place in our area, and though it had nothing whatever to do with the squadron, I think it is worth recording.

Early one morning, four German airmen walked into a village near Shaftesbury in Somerset and gave themselves up. The aeroplane which they must have come from could not be found anywhere. At about the same time a Dornier bomber made a perfect landing (without undercarriage) on the mud flats at Harwich nearly 130 miles away.

There were no crew in the Dornier and they could not be found. So, everybody at Harwich was saying "Where are the crew for this aeroplane" and everybody at Shaftesbury was saying "Where is the aeroplane for this crew". The puzzle was soon solved, and it is a rather amazing story.

The Dornier had left its base near Cherbourg en route for a raid on Liverpool and was flying up the West Country in very bad weather when it ran into a very heavy electrical storm near Shaftesbury. The machine was damaged by the storm and the pilot decided to abandon the raid and go home again.

So he turned about and flew south and somewhere in Somerset he ran into another storm with a very heavy electrical discharge and this completely upset their compass. They continued on their course, crossed the Channel and arrived safely over the French coast – almost home.

They then noticed that according to their compass they were steering due north, and obviously this is not the direction to fly if you want to get from England to France.

So, they turned back again and flew south on their compass, crossed the Channel again and saw the English coast beneath.

Obviously, this was the French coast, having flown south for so long. After a short time, as they could not find an aerodrome and were getting short of petrol, they baled out and walked to the nearest village to get help.

They were quite convinced that they were in France and one can imagine their mortification at finding themselves prisoners of war, particularly as they had already got home safely and then turned back again over enemy territory.

I bet they cursed that compass! Anyway, to finish the story, the Dornier flew along on its automatic pilot (or "George") and when the petrol ran out, it landed safely at Harwich.

This story is amazing, but absolutely true.

November 1940

At the beginning of November, the weather improved again and became brilliantly clear and cold, and the enemy took advantage of this weather and sent in some very strong fighter patrols towards Southampton and Portsmouth. They came over at immense heights – anything up to 35,000 feet – and were done with the sole intention of annoying us and killing as many as possible. No bombs were dropped, and they were merely offensive fighter patrols.

They certainly did annoy us, particularly because we were not able to get up to their height. The performance of the Messerschmitt is considerably lower than that of the Spitfire up to about 25,000 feet and after that the Messerschmitt has the advantage as it is fitted with a two-speed supercharger. Thus, we used to struggle painfully up to about 30,000 feet while they were buzzing around above us waiting to dive down and attack.

Fortunately, this failing of the Spitfires will soon be remedied as the new engines now coming into service have the two-speed supercharger fitted and, in fact, about two months ago, three of the new Spitfires met three Heinkel 113s at 38,000 feet and shot two of them down.

But in the autumn, we did not possess this advantage and so we flew about at 30,000 feet all the time, watching in painful suspense those blasted little Me. 109s playing about above us.

This sort of thing happened on several occasions at the beginning of November and though we did not have anybody killed, I think we were very lucky to get away with it. Fortunately, the German pilots showed very little determination to press home their advantage – if we had ever got to them in a similar position, they would have regretted it bitterly.

On November 1st, we took off to intercept a large enemy fighter patrol coming in towards Southampton. On this occasion we were trying to fly together with the Hurricanes of No. 238 Squadron as we thought that if we went out in large numbers it might make up for our disadvantage in height. But we found it rather difficult to keep formation with them as we were so much faster than their Hurricanes, so we passed underneath them and started to draw ahead.

Operations Room now called us up and said that we were very near the enemy. We all strained our eyes but could see nothing at all – by this time we were up at 32,000 feet and at that height the sky is very deep blue, and the glare of the sun is so strong that it completely dazzled you if you looked anywhere near it. Add to this the fact that, owing to the intense cold, our breath was condensing on the inside of the cockpit covering and then freezing so that it looked exactly like frosted glass, and you can imagine that we could scarcely see out at all. Not very pleasant when you know that at any moment a lot of Me. 109s may be dropping down on you from out of the sun, just like a ton of bricks!

Suddenly Novi, who had been flying at the back of the squadron with two others to guard our tails, let out a yell and we all turned round and saw the Hurricanes behind us diving away in all directions while about four Me. 109s, very conspicuous by their bright yellow noses, were climbing up rapidly into the blue again after their lightning attack. Obviously, the Hurricanes had been caught by surprise and we heard later that three of them had been shot down, though only one of them was killed.

We were very glad that we had decided to overtake them, or we should have been the rear squadron and caught it instead!

Altogether these affairs were not very pleasant as we could never ever relieve our feelings by letting off a few rounds at the Me. 109s, as they were always so far above us.

The next day, one section was ordered to take off and patrol Lyme Bay (just west of Weymouth) as a single enemy aircraft was approaching the coast. I took off, leading Green Section, and we went hard for Weymouth at about 15,000 feet.

We arrived over Lyme Bay, circled round and then Zurakowski shouted that he had seen a machine below. The Poles always seemed to see things first – they had marvellous eyes and knew how to use them. So, we dived after this machine on full throttle and started to overtake him very rapidly. As we got closer, I saw that it was a very large four engine bomber – we knew the Germans had some because they had been used occasionally against this country, but nobody had ever succeeded in shooting one down.

I was very excited – I was quite certain that we were going to be the first people in the R.A.F. to achieve this distinction! We were now in range and I was just about to open fire and let him have it when Hancock, who was flying No. 2, shouted "I think it's one of ours".

I took my thumb off the trigger and flew alongside whilst keeping out of range in case he should be hostile. To my amazement, there were red and blue roundels on the side – it was a Stirling!

Altogether a very good thing that Hancock stopped me because I was just about to fire and we should not have been very popular if we had destroyed one of our latest and largest bombers! Though it wouldn't have been our fault, as he had no business at all to be flying around the coast like that and Operations Room had told us definitely that he was a "bandit".

Anyway, all's well that ends well.

That night, I woke up in the early hours and listened very sleepily to the steady drone of a German bomber somewhere above us. This continued for a few minutes and then suddenly there was a very sharp hiss, followed by a thud and the tinkle of something breaking.

It sounded very close – far too close for my liking, and I got up and went out into the corridor where I found everybody else had been wakened and had got up to make enquiries. Everybody, that is, except

Michael, who had been fairly well bombed in London and was very bored by these proceedings in the middle of the night, so he stayed in bed.

Well, we found that a 250 lb delay action bomb had missed our wing in the mess by about 40 yards and had buried itself under the Salisbury-Andover road. It was far too close to the mess for our liking and altogether a very good job it didn't go off.

So, we all went to sleep on the other side of the building – all except Michael who sleepily announced that he intended to stay where he was and b- the bomb!

We had some more fun with the bomb later.

The next day, November 8th, was certainly one of the outstanding days of my life, though in the morning it seemed to be a very normal one.

For the last fortnight I had been ringing up D. every night and enquiring anxiously if young Nicholas was showing any signs of making his appearance in this world.

He was due any time after the first days of November but had apparently decided that there was no hurry, and poor D. used to announce sorrowfully every night that nothing had happened yet. So, we waited in hope.

Down at Wallop everything was very quiet in the morning, and we sat and talked and generally idled the time away till lunch. We went down to dispersal again in the afternoon and about 3.30 p.m. the Adjutant rang me up and said, "Do you know that you have been posted to Central Flying School, Upavon, for an instructor's course?"

This news absolutely staggered me, although I had known for the past few weeks that it was a possibility. The thought of leaving the squadron and all that grand crowd of people just depressed me beyond words.

About half an hour later an alarm came through and we all took off and made for Southampton. This was my last flight with the squadron and, by a curious coincidence, as both the C.O. and Frank

Howell were away, I led the squadron. I think I would have given ten years of my life then, to be able to meet some Huns and have a really good and successful fight. It would have been a glorious finish to my career in 609 to have led them in such an affair. But, alas, these last appearances are never as satisfactory as one could wish, and after about ten minutes flight we were ordered to land again. The enemy must have already turned back for France.

So, we returned to Wallop and I ordered the sections to land, while I stayed up for a few minutes on my own. I knew that this was my last flight in my beloved Spitfire, and I could not bring myself to land again and bid her farewell.

I climbed up to about 7,000 feet and came down in a long steep dive at nearly 500 m.p.h. and then went rocketing up again into an upward roll.

Up she went – round and up, with a great surge of power, just like the beautiful little thoroughbred that she was.

And thus, I bade farewell to my faithful companion of so many exciting days.

Half an hour later I walked into the mess and found a telegram waiting for me – "Dorothy fine son, everything ok, congratulations". So, Nicholas had arrived at last!

All my depression suddenly vanished, and I felt better and happier than I'd ever felt before.

That night we had the most terrific celebration party, firstly to greet the arrival of young Nicholas and secondly, as my farewell to the squadron.

At about ten o'clock we sallied forth from the mess and walked over to the NAAFI where a dance was in progress.

On the way over, Michael decided to have a look at the bomb, which was still lying under the road, though a hole had been dug down to it. So, we lifted the tarpaulin which covered the crater and Michael crawled down amidst cheers of encouragement and duly spat on the end of the bomb, after which we proceeded to the dance.

Next morning, I got up in very good time as I intended flying up to Huddersfield that day. Unfortunately, however, the weather was very bad and visibility practically nil so I had to wait all day at Wallop. In the afternoon I had my portrait done by Captain Orde, who was going round all the fighter squadrons drawing various pilots on behalf of the Air Ministry. That evening, we went into Andover and had dinner at the White Hart and early next morning I jumped out of bed and looked at the weather. It was clear at last!

So, I dressed hurriedly, had breakfast, said goodbye to everybody and took off in the Harvard for my journey north.

How I hated leaving the squadron! For 2½ years I had been in 609, starting with those grand weekends at Yeadon before the war, and the annual summer camp at Thorney Island or Church Fenton.

Looking back now, I see those glorious days as though outlined against a rapidly darkening background. Of the gay and light-hearted company of friends who flew together at Church Fenton in August 1939, more than half were killed within twelve months.

But in those days, none of us dreamt – or cared, I think – what lay ahead.

And what memories I have of 609 at war and in action! Starting with that memorable patrol over France and the unpleasant suspense of the day at Hawkinge; Drummond's death at Weymouth, and my first sight of the enemy, with the olive green colour of the Junkers 87, and the red flashes of my guns seen against the dark evening sky; the never-to-be-forgotten moment when the enemy machine burst into flames under my fire and plunged straight down into the sea many thousands of feet below, striking the water with a great spurt of white foam; the moment on the steps of the mess at Middle Wallop when I heard that Pip Barran and Gordon Mitchell had been killed that morning, and I felt so stunned that I could hardly think; our best fight of the war on August 13th, when we destroyed thirteen Huns in four minutes fighting; the battles over London in September and the spectacle of those enormous German formations droning steadily on despite the hail of fire to which they were subjected; that terrible minute when I walked into Glenwood on September 16th, and heard that Geoff was missing; ten days later flying home for his funeral and arriving late despite all my efforts; diving down just behind Mick Miller to attack a German formation and seeing him collide head-on with a Messerschmitt at 26,000 feet over Swanage; that glorious swoop at 600 m.p.h. to catch a diving Me. 109 on September 30th, and a few minutes later feeling rather sorry as I shot down another Me. 109 into the sea, so many miles from land; the suspense before we reached our 100, and the terrific celebrations that attended it; and the C.O. walking up to me and throwing the D.F.C. ribbon on my plate.

And then, too, there were the good friends I was leaving in the squadron – Noel Agazarian, Johnny Curchin, Frank Howell, Bishop, Overton, Novi and Osti, Forshaw and Hancock.

We had all been through so much together and had such good times. I think they were all about the best crowd of people I ever knew, and I felt very sad at having to part from them.

I flew north in very bad weather and landed at Kidlington near Oxford in order to refuel. After taking off again, I flew towards the east as the clouds were a little higher there, and I hit the L.N.E.R. line at Peterborough and came up the railway via Grantham, Doncaster and Wakefield.

I circled over Glenwood and did one or two rolls till I saw somebody waving from the lawn, and then I flew off to Yeadon where Father met me shortly afterwards. We drove over to Huddersfield and went straight to the nursing home.

I walked into the room and there were Dorothy and Nicholas waiting for me.

That was the best moment I had ever had, and I think it also marked the end of a very definite chapter – the happiest, the most gloriously exciting, and sometimes the most tragic six months of my life.

Epilogue

DMC was posted away from 609 Squadron, on 'rest' as an instructor, on 8 November 1940. He would not, in fact, return to operational flying.

Over the next few years, he served at the Central Flying School at Upavon, 15 Elementary Flying Training School at Carlisle, the Advanced Flying Units and Wheeton Aston and Ternhill, and 41 OTU, Hawarden. On 1 December 1944, he was posted to 8 (Coastal) OTU at Dyce, again flying Spitfires and providing photographic reconnaissance training.

On the morning of 18 December 1944, Flight Lieutenant Crook took off in a Spitfire Mk IX, EN662, on a training flight, but returned almost immediately to have a minor technical defect rectified. Taking off again and resuming the exercise, DMC would never return.

A Spitfire was seen to dive into the sea off Aberdeen from 20,000 feet, and a search of the area recovered flying clothing named to DMC. This brave and talented thirty-year-old pilot, a married man and father of two children, was never found. The cause of the crash is presumed to have been failure of the aircraft's oxygen supply system, rendering the pilot unconscious.

Flight Lieutenant David Moore Crook DFC is remembered on Panel 202 of the Runnymede Memorial, which commemorates 20,275 British and Commonwealth aircrew who have no known grave.

* * *

Inevitably, innumerable first-hand accounts emerged during and after the Second World War. Collectively, these provide an essential record of the human experience during that global conflagration, covering every theatre of war, every campaign and battle, as well as, I daresay, every role from auxiliary fireman to fighter pilot, and everything in between.

Fortunately, the air war has generated a vast amount of such literature, among which certain titles amongst which stand out. *The Last Enemy* by Flight Lieutenant Richard Hillary, a young Spitfire pilot badly burned during the Battle of Britain is widely lauded as a literary classic; Squadron Leader Brian Lane DFC's *Spitfire! The Experiences of a Fighter Pilot* would not be regarded a literary masterpiece, but it is certainly another superb account of flying, fighting and squadron life during the time of Dunkirk and the Battle of Britain; Wing Commander Ian 'Widge' Gleed DSO DFC's *Arise to Conquer* relates his experience flying Hurricanes throughout the same period. DMC's *Spitfire Pilot* must also surely be on any list of the very best wartime accounts. One chilling fact, thinking about it, is that all of the foregoing books were published in 1942 – and none of the authors survived the war.

With the initial edition of *Spitfire Pilot* having been published in 1942, and his novel *Pursuit of Passy* in 1946, DMC, the writer, will at least be remembered through his literary legacy – which is an important one. We can only surmise what David Crook might have gone on to achieve in the literary field had he survived.

Appendices

Appendix I

Flight Lieutenant D.M. Crook's Combat Reports

It is stated that on 9 July 1940, Crook destroyed a Junkers Ju 87 and damaged another. In action again on the 13th, he damaged a Dornier Do 17. On 11 August he destroyed a Messerschmitt Me 110, and on the 12th probably another. Then, on the 13th, Crook shot down a Messerschmitt Me. 109, on the 14th shared a Heinkel He 111, on 27th September shared a Me. 110 and on the 30th destroyed two Me. 109s and probably another.

The citation for the award of the Distinguished Flying Cross was published in *The London Gazette* on 1 November 1940. It states: 'This officer has led his section with coolness and judgment against the enemy on many occasions. He has destroyed six of their aircraft besides damaging several more.

The following, drawn from Air 50/171/15 (and published and licensed under the Open Government Licence v3.0.), are transcriptions of some of Crook's combat reports.

11 August 1940

Sector Serial No	(A)	Y105
Serial No. of Order Detailing Flight or Squadron to Patrol	(B)	A42
Date	(C)	11.8.40
Flight, Squadron	(D)	Flight B, Sqdn 609
Number of Enemy Aircraft	(E)	100 plus
Type of Enemy Aircraft	(F)	Me. 109 and Me. 110
Time Attack was delivered	(G)	About 1015 hours
Place Attack was delivered	(H)	15 miles S.S.E. of Swanage
Height of Enemy	(J)	15,000 to 30,000
Enemy Casualties	(K)	One Me. 110
Our Casualties, Aircraft	(L)	Nil
Personnel	(M)	Nil
Searchlights	(N1)	N/A
A.A.	(N2)	N/A
Range at which fire was opened and estimated length of burst	(P)	See text

GENERAL REPORT

P/O Crook Green 3. On sighting enemy Green 1 turned left and climbed hard into the sun. I was keeping very good lock-out behind, and Green 1 and 2 must have turned off to attack because I soon missed them.

A lot of Me. 110s were milling round below, and I saw one some little distance from the rest. I dived down on him and opened fire on a beam attack but could not get enough deflection owning to steepness of turn and this burst must have missed him. I then came out on his tail and so close that I had to throttle back to avoid collision. I gave him a good burst at practically point blank range and he turned to the right, appeared to stall, and started to turn over on his back.

I had to take violent evasive action to avoid hitting his left wing as he turned over. As there were a number of other enemy machines close to me I did not have time to see what happened to the Me. 110 which in view of my point-blank range and the fact that I saw my burst going right into the fuselage, I am fairly sure must have been destroyed.

Comment: Whereas Control told us before the action that our Angels (18) was adequate, we went into action at over 25,000 feet, and there were still some enemy aircraft above us.

12 August 1940

Sector Serial No	(A)	Y32
Serial No. of Order Detailing Flight or Squadron to Patrol	(B)	43
Date	(C)	12th August
Flight, Squadron	(D)	Blue 1, Flight B, Sqdn 609
Number of Enemy Aircraft	(E)	60 plus
Type of Enemy Aircraft	(F)	Me. 109, Me. 110, Ju 88
Time Attack was delivered	(G)	About 12.30
Place Attack was delivered	(H)	5 miles S. of Portsmouth
Height of Enemy	(J)	27,000
Enemy Casualties	(K)	1 Me. 110 probable
Our Casualties, Aircraft	(L)	Nil
Personnel	(M)	Nil
Searchlights	(N1)	N/A
A.A.	(N2)	N/A
Range at which fire was opened and estimated length of burst	(P)	–

GENERAL REPORT

I was Blue I took after the others as wireless was U.S. I climbed towards Isle of Wight and saw A.A. fire on my left over Portsmouth. Investigated but saw no bombers. Then saw three layers of enemy fighters milling round at between 22,000 and 26,000 ft off East end of Isle of Wight.

I climbed above middle layer which were Me. 110s, selected a target and dived down. I got in a short deflection burst and saw my bullets either hit him or go very close indeed to him. Narrowly avoided colliding and lost sight of him, and continued my dive down for perhaps another 3,000 ft when I pulled out.

At that moment an Me. 110 enveloped in a sheet of flame dived vertically past me within 200 yds. This machine was definitely destroyed, but I don't know whether it was mine or not. I think it quite possibly was as I could not see any other friendly fighters in action when I went down to attack.

I was in a very vulnerable position after pulling out of my dive as there were many enemy A/C round and above, so I dived at very high speed away from the area. On the way down I hit a violent bump which tore the landing lamp out of the wing.

27 September 1940

Sector Serial No	(A)	Y73
Serial No. of Order Detailing Flight or Squadron to Patrol	(B)	43
Date	(C)	27/9/40
Flight, Squadron	(D)	Flight B, Sqdn 609
Number of Enemy Aircraft	(E)	12–15
Type of Enemy Aircraft	(F)	Me. 110
Time Attack was delivered	(G)	1145
Place Attack was delivered	(H)	Swanage
Height of Enemy	(J)	25,000 ft.
Enemy Casualties	(K)	One Me. 110 destroyed
Our Casualties, Aircraft	(L)	Nil
Personnel	(M)	Nil
Searchlights	(N1)	N/A
A.A.	(N2)	Little and inaccurate firing during our attack.
Range at which fire was opened and estimated length of burst	(P)	–

GENERAL RPEORT

I was Blue 3, and our section got separated before the action took place. When we sighted the enemy Yellow section turned towards them to attack and I joined onto them. The enemy were flying round in an anti-clockwise circle, and I turned round to attack an Me. 110, but turned too tight and got into a spin.

When I climbed up again the circle was broken up and the enemy was streaming out to sea. I chased one Me. 110 and soon caught him. The gunner opened fire, but I gave him a burst and am sure that I killed him as there was no more fire.

I then emptied the rest of my ammunition into him, aiming at both engines in turn and the fuselage. Smoke poured from his port engine. I broke off the attack when I finished my ammunition, and P/O Bisdee came in and finished him off.

30 September 1940

Sector Serial No	(A)	Y74
Serial No. of Order Detailing Flight or Squadron to Patrol	(B)	–
Date	(C)	30/9/40
Flight, Squadron	(D)	B, 609 Squadron
Number of Enemy Aircraft	(E)	6–7
Type of Enemy Aircraft	(F)	Me. 109
Time Attack was delivered	(G)	11.30
Place Attack was delivered	(H)	Swanage
Height of Enemy	(J)	23,000 feet.
Enemy Casualties	(K)	2 Me. 109 destroyed
Our Casualties, Aircraft	(L)	–
Personnel	(M)	–
Searchlights	(N1)	–
A.A.	(N2)	–
Range at which fire was opened and estimated length of burst	(P)	–

GENERAL REPORT

I was Green 1, and shortly before the action started, Sorbo Leader ordered us into line astern Blue Section. A moment later a few Me. 109s flew across in front of us at about the same height.

We all turned round after them and the enemy started to dive. I followed one down, at some distance behind him, but my speed went up to about 600 m.p.h. and I caught him easily, coming up from below and astern as he flattened out of his dive. I gave him a good burst and he turned over streaming smoke and dived into the sea.

This was witnessed by Sgt. Feary.

As I finished firing at him, I saw an Me. 109 on my right, more or less break up in mid-air. This was P/O Appleby's victim.

I then chased another Me. 109 out towards France and soon caught him. I gave him a good burst, his cockpit covering came off and flashed right past my head, and he turned over and dived. To my amazement he flattened out before hitting the water, and climbed up again though he was streaming glycol smoke behind him.

I caught him up again and made no mistake this time. He went into the sea about 25 miles from the French coast.

Appendix II

"The Americans"

The following text relating to the presence of American pilots on 609 (West Riding) Squadron is taken from the first edition of *Spitfire Pilot*:

These three Americans – "Andy", "Shorty", and "Red", had come over to join the French Air Force. They reached France in May just at the beginning of the German attack, and when things started to crack up they hitch-hiked down to Saint-Jean-de-Luz and got away in the last ship, without being able to get accepted by the French. In London they got a pretty cool reception at the American Embassy, who obviously weren't going to assist them to break the neutrality laws. They even tried to send them back to the States.

But fortunately Red had got an introduction to some M.P. and went along to the House to see him. After that everything went smoothly; twenty-four hours later they were in the R.A.F., and after a short training they came to us. They had been civil pilots in America and had done a lot of flying. But civil flying is one thing and military flying, particularly in war, is quite another, and they were very raw and inexperienced when they came to us. However, they were keen, and soon improved.

They were typical Americans, amusing, always ready with some devastating wisecrack (frequently at the expense of authority), and altogether excellent company. Our three Yanks became quite an outstanding feature of the squadron.

Andy was dark, tough, and certainly rather good-looking with his black hair and flashing eyes.

Red was very tall and lanky, and possessed the most casual manner and general outlook on life that I ever saw. I don't believe he ever batted an eyelid about anything, except possibly the increasing difficulty of getting his favourite "rye high". After a fight he never showed the slightest trace of excitement, and I remember that after one afternoon's fairly concentrated bombing of the aerodrome, during which a number of people were killed, he turned up grinning as usual but with his clothes in an awful mess and covered in white chalk because he had to throw himself several times into a chalk pit as the Huns dropped out of the clouds. He made only the grinning comment, "Aw hell, I had a million laffs!"

Shorty was the smallest man I ever saw, barring circus freaks, but he possessed a very stout size in hearts. When he arrived in the squadron we couldn't believe that he would ever reach the rudder bar in a Spit; apparently the Medical Board thought the same and refused to have him at first, as he was much shorter than the R.A.F. minimum requirements. However, Shorty insisted on having a trial, and he produced two cushions which he had brought all the way from the States via France, specially for this purpose. One went under his parachute and raised him up, the other he wedged in the small of his back, and thus he managed to fly a Spitfire satisfactorily, though in the machine all you could see of him was the top of his head and a couple of eyes peering over the edge of the cockpit.

Appendix III

A Report In The Times

The following text represents a footnote that was included in the first edition of *Spitfire Pilot*:

From *The Times*, 28th September 1940: "At one time bombers with escorting fighters crossed the Dorset coast in two waves each of at least fifty machines. They were hotly attacked by A.A. fire and R.A.F. fighters and six were seen to fall in flames.

"One had a direct hit from an A.A. shell and exploded in the air. Three crashed west of Poole and another fell into the sea. The funerals of four German airmen who were killed in an air battle two days ago were taking place during yesterday's air battle." (This statement is not quite correct. The enemy aircraft seen to explode in the air was actually the collision between Mick and the Me. 110, but as it happened at about 27,000 feet the onlookers on the ground naturally could not see exactly what occurred)

Appendix IV

609 Squadron's Successes

The following text relating to 609 (West Riding) Squadron's achievements, and a supporting footnote, is taken from the first edition of *Spitfire Pilot*:

> The actual score was 100 enemy aircraft definitely destroyed, a big number probably destroyed, and many more damaged. This meant a loss of about 300 German airmen killed or captured, and against this our own losses were thirteen pilots killed.[1]

---

1. The following report appeared in the *Yorkshire Post*: 'A Yorkshire Auxiliary Air Force fighter squadron has shot down 100 enemy planes, states the Air Ministry News Service. The 100th victim was a Junkers 88 bomber, which was sent plunging earthwards over the South Coast.

    'The squadron has fought with distinction at Dunkirk, in the Channel battles, and in the defence of London and the cities of South and West. Over Dunkirk, nine of the Spitfires shot down in one day four bombers and two Messerschmitt 109s.

    'One day, near Portland, within the space of a few minutes, they shot down nine Junkers 87 dive-bombers and four Messerschmitt 109s. This victory was achieved without loss.

    'During the first big raid on London the pilots shot down two Messerschmitt 110s, a Dornier 17, and a Messerschmitt 109 – again without loss.

    'One of the pilots, when over Southampton, was the first to attack a formation of 70 bombers. At the end of half an hour the raiders had been driven off with the loss of 15 bombers and 16 fighters.'

Bibliography

Crook, D.M., *Spitfire Pilot*, Faber & Faber Ltd, London, 1942

——, *Spitfire Pilot*, Grub Street, London, 2008

——, *Pursuit of Passy*, Herbert Joseph, London, 1946

Ellan, B.J., *Spitfire! Experiences of a Fighter Pilot*, John Murray Ltd, London, 1942

Gleed, I., *Arise to Conquer*, Victor Gollancz Ltd, London, 1942

Hillary, R., *The Last Enemy*, MacMillan & Co Ltd, London, 1942

Sarkar, D., *The Few: The Story of the Battle of Britain in the Words of the Pilots*, Amberley Publishing Ltd, Stroud, 2009

——, *Battle of Britain 1940: The Finest Hour's Human Cost*, Pen & Sword Ltd, Barnsley, 2020

Ziegler, F., *The Story of 609 Squadron: Under the White Rose*, MacDonald & Co (Publishers) Ltd, London, 1971

Other Books by Dilip Sarkar
(In order of publication)

Index